Half-Hours With My "Guide"

The Writings of Elizabeth Swift Brengle

Half-Hours with My "Guide"

The Salvation Army Supplies
Atlanta, GA USA

The Writings of Elizabeth Swift Brengle:

Volume One • Half-Hours With My "Guide"
Volume Two • The Army Drum
Volume Three • What Hinders You?
Volume Four • Biography by Eileen Douglas

Half-Hours With My "Guide"

Copyright © 1990 by The Salvation Army
ISBN: 0-86544-057-3
Printed in the United States of America

First Printing, June 1990

Available through bookstores and Salvation Army
Supplies or through the Publisher.

The Salvation Army Supplies and Purchasing Dept.
1424 Northeast Expressway
Atlanta, Georgia 30329

Contents

Preface

Human life is lived day by day; and to be guided along the right way for soul, mind, and body is the chief necessity of our existence. There are few who have not known the need of counsel in the ordinary perplexities of life, and fewer still who have not learned the unstableness of their own will and the trouble into which their natural inclinations draw them. Some are plunged into the deeps in which they find themselves helpless; their perseverance sickens, hope fails, and their hearts grow faint before an adversity which thwarts every endeavor and seems destined to last until their breath is spent. With others success gilds everything earthly with the appearance of true gold, worldly pleasure deafens the spiritual ear, and thought and time are consumed on that which is both fleeting and unsubstantial.

The Salvation Army believes and teaches that the main object in life should be to serve and glorify God. Before and above every other aim and duty is that of saving souls. Many of the ills that afflict mankind arise from the neglect of this supreme obligation. To save our own souls there must be a forsaking of sin, and a real belief in Christ; to help others there must be constant prayer, toil, and self-sacrifice, as well as a daily consecration to the doing of the will of God. The Bible, which is one of His chosen means of making known His will, contains an unfailing source of perfect wisdom—sufficient to help us in every possible difficulty which may arise. None can be a conquering Soldier of Jesus Christ without constant communication with God by prayer. No life can really glorify God if He does not con-

7

trol every thought and govern every action; and no life that He does control, and govern, will be a failure.

These truths are set forth in this book, which is a companion and supplement to "The Salvation Soldier's Guide," which, as our late General explained at the time of its publication:

> Was never meant in any degree to take the place of the Bible, which every true Salvation Soldier so highly values.
>
> It is intended in these days of all but universal doubting and coldness towards God and man, to declare anew and confirm your devotion to all God's written revelation. . . .
>
> What we want to promote is the daily reading of all parts of the Bible, instead of that preference for the New Testament which we find more and more common where men hope to make the name of Jesus Christ a sort of shelter for unbelief and sin.

Readers who are not Salvationists will find teaching in these pages on the subject of Holiness, which is at the same time one of The Army's greatest joys and strengths.

The book is issued in the hope that it will increase the faith and knowledge of the faithful, and encourage many to a closer study of the precious Volume.

Can You Say "I *Know*"?

And the earth was without form, and void; and darkness was upon the face of the deep. And the Spirit of God moved upon the face of the waters (Gen. 1:2).

It is always the work of the Spirit of God to bring order out of chaos, light out of darkness, definiteness out of indefiniteness, certainty out of uncertainty, a clear experience out of a mixed state of the affections and will.

My comrade, does your spiritual experience somewhat resemble the primal earth? Is it shapeless when compared with the well rounded, clean-cut religious life of some Christians you know; void of the triumphant experience of Salvation which they possess; and with gloom and deep shadows where there should be an unbroken flood of light? The Holy Spirit is continually brooding over you, moving over the God-created deeps of your heart, to change this unhappy state of things, and to bring your experience to that condition of which even the Father Himself shall say that it is "good"; say even to you, as He did of some of His earliest servants, "He walked before Me with a perfect heart."

A man ought to be as sure of his Salvation from sin as of his existence. There is no foundation in the Bible for a "hope-so" religion; everything about Salvation in it is as clear and practicable and demonstrable as a proposition in Euclid.

"These things have I written unto you that believe on

9

the name of the Son of God," wrote John, addressing Christians, "that ye may *know*" (not guess, or think, or hope, or even believe, but "know") "that ye have eternal life." The evidences are as plain as possible; apply them to your experience, and if you have eternal life, you will know it just as well as those early Christians knew it who went joyfully to the lions or to the stake that they might enter into its unhindered possession. You will then not be scared out of your knowledge by men or devils, by arguments without or doubts within; you will laugh at all efforts to controvert your positive knowledge.

Read the things that John says "we know" in his very positive Epistles. John does not take his stand on a lonely height of spiritual pre-eminence, and say, "I know these things"; but joins himself in the most matter-of-course way with the rank and file of God's children everywhere, as if it were the very A B C of Salvation to know them. "We know that we are of God"; "We know that the Son of God is come"; "We know that we have the petitions that we desire of Him"; "Hereby know we that we dwell in Him, and He in us"; "We have known and believed the love that God hath to us"; "We know that He abideth in us"; "We know that we have passed from death unto life"; "We know that we are of the truth."

Have you this knowledge, comrade? Have you let God finish His fair creation of purity; and peace in your heart, or do you find yourself by doubts and fears and sins again and again going back to chaos in your soul, only to begin once more to place yourself in line with His design for you by a fresh repentance?

The Spirit of God is brooding over you always, to help you, to teach you, to carry you ever forward, to finish the work of your Salvation, and set you developing for all time and eternity. You will never progress in your religious life till you become positive about your own state.

The Bible "hope" is a "sure" one; a "lively hope," and

not the "trembling hope" which some professed Christians speak of, which is only a doubt in disguise. Make sure of yours by the Bible process of believing God, till you can exchange its faint expression for that triumphant cry of Paul's, "I *know* whom I have believed."

The Lust of the Eyes

And when the woman saw that the tree was good for food, and that it was pleasant to the eyes, and a tree to be desired to make one wise, she took of the fruit thereof, and did eat, and gave also unto her husband with her; and he did eat (Gen. 3:6).

Eve did not sin ignorantly; very few people do. She had learned her lesson of obedience well, and even recited it to the Devil. "God hath said!" There was the commandment. We Christians accept our Bible as God's word, the whole of it; but before how many different precepts and orders has He put the danger-signal, "God hath said!" Like children, we need emphasis as well as repetition, and God gives us plenty of it.

But our first mother forgot her orders through chatting with an improper companion, and listening to the talk and argument of a person who was not subject to her Lord. Do you?

Then, here is warning number one for you, floating down from the very beginning of earthly temptation and sorrow, to find listening ears. Will it find such in you? Do not parley with the Devil, or his agents. Tell what God has said, and then turn away from those who will not mind Him, and obey Him yourself. The French proverb, "The garrison which parleys, the woman who listens, is going to surrender," may well be applied to Christian experience. Neither argue with nor listen to those who deny God's truth; deliver your "God hath said," and go. It is a tremendous thought that if Eve had only followed this simple plan, you might have enjoyed life in happy innocence! And if you go down like Eve before temptation, you are bound to entail misery on those dear to you; and on how many poor struggling souls who can tell?

Eve went on. Listening to temptation, entertaining instead of spurning it, she opened the avenue of all her senses to selfish and hellish suggestions. She considered her palate. She had plenty of good, wholesome food, was healthy and satisfied from its use; but now she wanted to gratify her appetite at the expense of her conscience. One often hears the question asked, "Why do you eat that rich food? Don't you know it will make you ill?" and answered, "I don't suppose it's good for me, but I'm so fond of it."

Such people, from Eve down, have got at least one ear open to the Devil. "What! know ye not that your body is the temple of the Holy Ghost which is in you?" and "If any man defile the temple of God, him shall God destroy."

Eve had not the scientific knowledge of food values and hygienic eating which are open to very common people nowadays. She had never heard of over-eating, of unwholesome dainties, of dyspepsia, so she stands clear before God from the sin of gluttony—of eating what "tastes good," and that to excess, instead of eating as Daniel did—for strength to serve God with body and mind.

"Eat to live, and that in the highest sense," is the second warning that floats down to you from the beginning of centuries.

Eve looked at the forbidden fruit. She had no business to do that. Neither have we. The eyes should be kept from evil things, lest they tempt the heart to sin. Job "made a covenant" with his eyes, and so must every Christian. Very few sanctified souls can look at the pretty but needless things in shop windows as they used to do before God cleansed their hearts from covetousness. They can only do it upon necessary occasions, without the "lust of the eyes" creeping back to lead them to spend their money (of which they are only stewards) unwisely, or to desire what they cannot, or ought not to, buy. "Turn away mine eyes from beholding vanity," prayed the man whose eyes once led him into "the lowest hell" of sin and iniquity; and again, "I will set no wicked thing before mine eyes." He did not mean to expose himself to temptation. The Devil gets an easy victory when we stop to look at forbidden fruit. More than once in the old days of sinfulness I sighed, "O Eve, why didn't you go?"

"Why didn't *I* go?"—"Why don't *you* go?" These questions are more to the purpose.

"Mine eyes are ever toward the Lord," sang the restored David. Then they could not tempt him. We cannot look at God and at the sinful things at the same time. "Ever toward the Lord" is the only safe way.

"Don't look where you cannot see God" is the third lesson borne down to us on the wings of years from the talk in the Garden of Eden.

Eve had an unhealthy thirst for knowledge. That is, she wanted to pry into things which God did not think good for her, a knowledge which would make her less pleasing and less useful to Him. Oh, what a pitifully large family she has growing upon the earth! Head knowledge that crowds out God, that seeks to disprove or nullify the one great fact of our lives, abounds among the peoples of every nation. Satan is always ready to make human knowledge appear desirable, especially when it tends to stop the glorious work of saving souls. All knowledge-seekers have a lesson to learn from their race-mother's costly failure in acquiring it. "Whether there be knowledge, it shall vanish away."

"The fear of the Lord is the beginning of knowledge";

but Eve put aside her godly fear when she sought a cheap and quick education. Do not commit her blunder.

Paul, on the other hand, sold his life for the "excellency of the knowledge of Christ," and God created you that you might have the knowledge of His glory in Christ Jesus.

And so the last warning which comes down from the primal day when a human being first put her head before her heart is this: "Know God at all costs."

Joy Given, Not Sold

But unto Cain and to his offering He had not respect.
And Cain was very wroth, and his countenance fell.
And the Lord said unto Cain, Why art thou wroth?
and why is thy countenance fallen? If thou doest well,
shalt thou not be accepted? and if thou doest not
well, sin lieth at the door (Gen. 4:5-7).

I once saw a girl go out to the Penitent-Form weeping and trembling. She knelt there long, and came away quiet; but, except that, as the days went on, a look of furtive resentment crept into her face, and gradually settled on it, there was no change in her.

Then the truth came out. She was a backslider, and she wanted her old, happy experience again. She had sought God merely to regain it, and had come away from the Penitent-Form as dissatisfied as she went there. She had not sought first His righteousness. She had not fulfilled the conditions, and yet, like Cain, was angry because God did not reward an outward act which had no reference to her inward state of soul towards Him. She did "not well," sin still lay at her door, and sin and happiness cannot exist together in the soul. "If thou doest well, shalt thou not be accepted?"

It is wonderful that people will keep on claiming God's promises without any regard to the conditions which are invariably prefixed, and then, like Cain, complain angrily, "God does not hear!" "The Bible is not true," "There is no use in praying."

That girl was not deeply convicted of sin. She did not want to be like Jesus; she only remembered the sweet joy she had known as a Christian; she could not find it in the world. So she sought to purchase it by an outward act of submission at the Penitent-Form.

But God does not sell His great possessions. He gives His Spirit freely, "without measure," to those who become His children, and one of the fruits of the Spirit is joy. Joy, we repeat, is only given to God's child, not sold to a sinner.

The lack of happiness in sin, and the boundless measure of it to be found in serving God, are strong incentives for a sinner to seek Christ. But if he does not lose sight of these motives when he gets so near to God as kneeling at the Penitent-Form ought to bring him, there is something wrong with his spiritual eyesight. It needs correcting by a look to Jesus as the Savior from sin. He needs to think about the true meaning of repentance.

"How can I repent, if thinking of my sins does not make me feel bad?" has been asked by one of these present-day Cains.

Pray for repentance. Read how the sinners of Wesley's time had their needs sung out before them, till many realized them for themselves, and got made into stalwart saints:

> Oh, that I could repent!
>   Oh, that I could believe!
> Thou by Thy voice the marble rend,
>   The rock in sunder cleave!

Oh, that I could revere
My much offended God!
Oh, that I could but stand in fear
Of Thy afflicting rod!

If mercy cannot draw,
Then by Thy threatenings move
And keep an abject soul in awe,
That will not yield to love.

If you do not feel real conviction, and real repentance, with which to come before God, ask Him, ask Him with all your heart, and His love will supply it.

"Go, and I Will Bless Thee"

Now the Lord had said unto Abram, Get thee out of thy country, and from thy kindred, and from thy father's house, unto a land that I will show thee: and I will make of thee a great nation, and I will bless thee, and make thy name great; and thou shalt be a blessing: and I will bless them that bless thee, and curse them that curseth thee: and in thee shall all families of the earth be blessed (Gen. 12:1-3).

It is wonderful to think what a covenant God here makes with us! Yes, with us: for the promises were "to Abraham and his seed," and we are "the children of Abraham by faith." "So then, they which be of faith are blessed with faithful Abraham" (Gal. 3: 8,9).

The conditions are plain and easy to fulfil; far easier for us than for our great father in the faith. With us the getting out from our country and kindred and father's house is, for the most part, figurative, spiritual proceeding; and also we have a larger measure of the Spirit than had been poured out upon men in that far-back dispensation. It is a tremendous thought, when we look at the continual and vast sacrifices of Abraham in obeying God, that God has a right to expect more of us than of him, because of our far greater degree of privilege!

The conditions are these: total separation in spirit from the world, which is opposed to God, even if it includes our nearest and dearest on earth, and a strict following of the path that God shows us. At the time of Abraham's call, God did not show him the promised land—did not give him a map or description of it, or even its name—but exacted a prospective, as well as present, obedience. We speak sometimes of surrendering "all we know, and all we do not know"; that was what Abraham had to do. He had to trust God for all the particulars of the future; he could not be sure that the land was as good as the one he left; that it had not hard winters and summers of drought; he only knew that it was the land of God's choice for him.

Is that enough for a soul to know? If Abraham could only come back and tell us! But Abraham has spoken out of Paradise, and told us that if we do not believe God, neither would we believe if one rose from the dead. And yet, even that help to our faith has been granted to *us*—Jesus rose from the dead, and told us, with almost His last spoken words, to "go." "Where?" "Into all the world," He said to His Church collectively. To the individual His words mean, "Unto the land that He will show thee."

First of all, that land has a spiritual significance; you must enter into the land of "rest from inbred sin"; and then if there is a further, outward path, you will be fit to travel in it. It may be India, it may be only the nearest Corps; God will show you; you have only to go.

The going is our part. Now look at God's part. "I will bless thee." In that blessing lies the bliss you have been seeking for years, but have never found. It is almost impossible to explain to one who does not know what marvels lie hidden under the name of God's blessing. Dr. Steele, a lion of American Methodism, calls his experience of this Canaan blessing, "years on wings"; and the saints of Wesley's day used such expressions as "weighted with bliss," "filled with God," "full of His glory." God's people have exhausted language in trying to depict the joys He bestows upon His obedient children; and finding the task beyond their power, they say with Nathanael, "Come, and see."

"I will make thee a blessing." Saved people always want to pass on their joy, and to see other people born again. But after a certain period, unless they advance in their experience to sanctification, their best efforts fail; their mouths are shut and tongues tied by a secret sense of sin in their own hearts. They keep on wishing, but wishing in vain, to get others saved.

Get the blessing of a clean heart, and God will make you a blessing in turn. Meet the conditions, and the heavens shall pass away before His word shall fail: "I will make thee a blessing."

There is one part of the covenant that looks at first sight to be for Abraham only; but it surely is for us in our degree. "In thee shall all families of the earth be blessed." Jesus came once in the flesh through Abraham's line; and in that way He will not come again. But when God has His perfect, undisputed way with you, it will please Him to reveal His Son in you as He did in Paul. Then you will know that you have a share in this clause of the covenant, and the world will be better, will be blessed, because of you.

Guard the Children

And the servant said unto him, Peradventure the woman will not be willing to follow me unto this land: must I needs bring thy son again unto the land from whence thou camest? And Abraham said unto him, Beware thou that thou bring not my son thither again (Gen. 24:5, 6).

Abraham throws every possible safeguard about his child to keep him from the influence of that world whose deadening effect upon the soul he had known in his own boyhood and early manhood. Is this the course generally followed by religious people of today in the Church or even in The Salvation Army? There are some who do so, and may God multiply them!

There was no religious society in Abraham's day outside his own tents, and so he kept Isaac wandering up and down the land, not permitting friendly relations with any possible neighbors; and when the time came for his marriage, he looked out for a wife who would help him to serve God.

Eliezer evidently had not his master's faith, and wanted to "lay at anchor to windward" in the shape of a heathen wife, in case of possible failure to secure the right kind. But Abraham twice lays on him the strict command, "Beware thou that thou bring not my son thither again." Better no wife at all than a worldly one. Amen, Abraham!—much better! Witness the scores of men dragged down from a high plane of godliness and service for souls by a world-loving, world-seeking, ambitious wife!

We cannot rule or even guide our children nowadays quite to the age of Isaac when God gave him Rebecca. But it should be easily possible to train them to love God so much better than any of His works, that they will never put any of His creatures before Him—never even think

19

seriously of marrying one who would hinder instead of help their walk with God.

A mother who had done this told me that her son had carried his clean heart intact through two colleges, but in the course of his ministerial work was much thrown into the company of a beautiful, fascinating girl, not fully saved, whose preference for him was easy to see. His mother's fears were roused at last to the point of plain speaking.

"I told him," she said, "that education was desirable, and that a finished musician would be of great help to him in his work, but that I would rather see him take a wife who could not read or write than one who was not fully saved. He satisfied me, however, for he said that he never had any other thought; that he loved God too well to be happy with a wife who had not all the Salvation that God had for her in this world."

I knew how this mother had trained her son for God all his life, and how he had taken in the idea "God first" with his earliest thoughts. So, on reaching an age when she had to set him entirely free from control, he, of his own accord, wanted still "God first."

Keep the children from evil while it is in your power. Seek for them the same heavenly blessings you seek for yourself. Abjure for them the same temptations to evil which you avoid yourself. The world's praise and admiration never brought you anything but disappointment and vexation; why would you want them for your little ones? You have given up the world's fashions for yourself, as un-Christian and injurious to your soul; is it not the height of foolish inconsistency to allow them for your children? You have had to put away the world's amusements and veneer as quick poison to your spiritual life; how dare you let your children learn to love them? You have found all the world's ways bitter and death-dealing to yourself, and yet you let your children slip into them! Do you think that the thorns will stop growing, the Devil cease tempting, the law of God alter for them?

No, they will say in the future, as you have in the past—

> Woe's me, that easy way we went!
> So bitter when we would return!

And maybe they will never find the grace that you did to escape from off its Hellward slope.

If you are a Christian, you are one who had come out from the world, and Abraham, the friend of God, cries down the ages to all such, "Beware thou that thou bring not *thy* son thither again."

The Exercise of Faith

And he said, Let me go, for the day breaketh. And he said, I will not let thee go, except thou bless me (Gen. 32:26).

Persistence is a marked characteristic of true faith, and it is a quality which God encourages, all through His word.

Why should God wish us to keep on asking, and urging our claim on Him, when He seems to deny us? Is it not a sort of setting up of our will against His?

No, not at all; it is rather a falling in with His expressed will.

I saw a wise mother exercising her baby once, to give him strength. She put a bright apple before his wondering eyes, as he lay stretched out upon the floor, and instantly the idle muscles put themselves to work to reach it. When baby had squirmed and wriggled himself nearly up to it, his mother moved the apple away a bit, and so he followed the pretty thing across the carpet, till she thought he had had the right amount of exercise, and then she let the fat hands reach and hold it.

Exercise is a necessity for life and health in spiritual things as well as physical; and faith, the spiritual hand by which our soul grasps the promises, without exercise can have no strength, cannot grow. As the baby would have lacked something if it had gotten the apple at the first effort, so faith would in the end grow lank and weak, like a hot-house plant, if its prayers were all answered immediately, and the promises fulfilled at the first asking.

Faith is often half-hearted, but the soul does not perceive this until a seeming denial comes. Then it realizes its great need, and is stirred up to a whole-hearted, desperate effort. Then it will come to an All-Night of Prayer like Jacob, and will cling to God with a hold that will not relax, and which the tender, yearning, Divine Love will never seek to break.

The soul has certain God-given rights in its Savior. It has a right to a cleansed nature, to perfect love, to the likeness of Jesus. These rights are in God's hands, to be taken from them by faith. But in most cases for years they lie there waiting! Some violent Esau must come against the soul, some dense thunder-cloud blacken its sky, before it feels its need of a mightier strength wherewith to weather the storm. The time of trial makes the need plain, stirs up the soul to the insistence which God longs to see in it, and develops; the faith necessary to obtain blessings from Him.

"Let me go," said the Savior, acknowledging by the words His inability to leave a soul which clung to Him by faith, and claimed its cross-bought rights. Wonderful and pregnant fact—that God submits Himself to a persistent faith! Short has said, "All Heaven is free plunder to faith."

All God's dealing with us are with a view to establish our faith. Jacob's sin had found him out after many years, but the very finding threw him desperately upon God for forgiveness and deliverance from it. Sometimes our carnal natures have to bring us face to face with death or despair, before we realize their relation to the Devil, and our absolute need to be freed from them. Thus Divine Love turns our very sins to account by bringing us to that condition of soul that earnestly desires and seeks Full Salvation; only demanding in return, that we shall constantly obey and persistently believe.

Emmanuel

And the Lord was with Joseph; and he was a prosperous man (Gen. 32:2).

We Salvationists ought never to mistake or forget the true standards of life; they are to be found only in our Bibles. The standard of earthly prosperity is here set up—it consists in having God with us. In the prison and in the palace alike, God was with Joseph, "And that which he did the Lord made it to prosper."

The life of Joseph is a most practical illustration of the saying of our Lord, that "the meek shall inherit the earth." Joseph was a pure-hearted, godly man, fully saved, and with a grand faith in God; and wherever he went, God gave him "the earth." When he became Potiphar's steward, wealth flowed for Potiphar into Joseph's hands; when he became a prisoner, all the authority and freedom of the Governor were his by depute; when he came into Pharaoh's employ, much of the power and privilege of government were given over to him.

Joseph is not the only believer who has proved that "godliness is profitable unto all things, having promise of the life that now is, and of that which is to come." The promises have not yet run out; the trouble is, to find people who will claim them. I remember yet the man who came rushing up to the Congress Hall, London, in my Cadet days, to tell the slum lasses that God had answered his prayer. He had told Him how he needed work, and God had kept His promises and sent it—a good job, that bid fair to last all the winter. Within twenty-four hours after he had let God be "with him," he made a beginning of prosperity.

Give to Jesus Glory

And Joseph answered Pharaoh, saying, It is not in me: God shall give Pharaoh an answer of peace (Gen. 41:16).

Joseph might have preserved a modest silence when Pharaoh spoke of his gift of interpretation, and so have received the glory without using any sinful words. But he had no idea of taking credit to himself in any way. Self had died in the prison, and when the praise of man came searching Joseph out, it found nothing in him to respond to it. He disclaimed any power in himself, but attributed it all to his God; there was to be no mistake on Pharaoh's part as to who could interpret his mysterious dream.

Self in Joseph had been severely crushed years back, when he had bid for the praise of his brothers by telling the dreams of his own superiority. It had won for him exile, slavery, and a prison: and it took thirteen years of bondage to starve out that praise-hungry self, and put God on His rightful throne in Joseph's heart. Who but God would have such patience with us, and work so long, so ingeniously, so variously, to put us in the way of real happiness?

You, too, comrade, must give God the glory. Is there a

secret longing in your heart to "know what people think of you," especially if the opinion is likely to be a favorable one? Is there a hungering in your spirit for people's approval of your work, your sacrifices, your consecrated abilities? Get rid of these things as you would of a nest of baby vipers. Take your longings to Jesus, and let Him satisfy you. Jesus alone is worthy; He only has ever done anything in this mortal vale to merit glory and honor. Join in the chorus of praise to Him which all the redeemed in Heaven are singing, and see how quickly these devilish thoughts of self-praise will vanish.

God has warned us clearly to give glory to Him "before He causes darkness, and before your feet stumble upon the dark mountains." When we seek praise, or covet glory, we are looking away from Jesus, the Light; and look away from Him is to look straight into the dark. Beware, then, lest "while ye look for light" (in self) "He turn it into the shadow of death, and make it gross darkness"—utter backsliding.

Recognize the fact that all your virtue, your powers, your graces, your faith, all that you are and have, are things lent to you; then, as a poor borrower, do not glory, but give praise to the gracious, glorious Lender.

None of Self

For God hath made me forget all my toil, and all my father's house (Gen. 41:51).

Salvationists have no time and no inclination for heresy-hunting, but Joseph's God-honoring statement in this verse is so often controverted by other religionists that we are glad to point out, for once, the difference between their creed and the Bible.

Joseph says here plainly, "God satisfies me wholly"; the heretical people say, "If God would give me certain things I should be happy." Joseph's doctrine is sound, Scriptural, and eternally true; the other doctrine is false and rotten to the core.

"Mrs. Blank is very happy," said a sceptic to a Christian.

"Yes," was the answer. "Who would not be, with a home like hers?"

"Oh, but I meant in her religion. She always seems full of it, and so happy in it."

"Yes, in her home," was repeated, "Anybody could be happy with the family surroundings she has. Why shouldn't she be happy?"

"I always give religion credit for it," said the sceptic again, and the subject passed. But that unbeliever had heard heresy from the lips of a Christian—had been taught by plain inference that God does not satisfy the hearts of His children, but that His gifts could, and did!

The Bible upholds Joseph's creed, our hymns repeat it, the testimony of myriad witnesses supports it, the great facts of spiritual life are in accord with it. God does satisfy, "though all His gifts remove." Glory to His name for ever!

"God hath made me forget," said Joseph; and he set up a living monument to his Savior's goodness in his son's name, after the goodly old-time fashion. It was God who drew the soft veil of forgetfulness over his sorrowful past—God, not Asenath and her boys, not the proud home in which he could keep them, not Egyptian air or pagan power—it was God, his Savior. He did not say, "My home is better than my father's tents; this Southern princess and her flower-like babies are better housemates than my jealous, quarrelsome brothers." He declared, instead, that God was better than father, kindred, and native land; that Salvation was better than anything earth had to offer; that God was enough for him

In his prison Joseph had learned a lesson in proportionate values. He had found, when "his should come into iron" (Psalm 55:18, margin), that the only true freedom was a spiritual one, and he found his freedom in God. He had found that the tenderest earthly relationships, except as they reflect the love of God in the human soul, bring as much pain as joy, and can never satisfy. So he yielded all his powers of loving into a heart-following of his Savior, content to use them for the blessing of others as God should direct. The self-life of Joseph died in that Egyptian prison, and from henceforth he could say, "I live, yet not I; but Christ liveth in me."

This is not mystical talk; it is the plainest possible expression of the experience of entire sanctification. Any one who has passed through the strait gate of death to self, and come out into the broad, golden plains of life in Jesus, knows what happened to Joseph in his prison, and can say with him, "God hath made me forget all my toil"—all the losses, the sorrows, the bitter "works without faith," the stinging, piercing death-in-life service—and "all my father's house"—the disappointments, the grievings, the feeding of the human heart upon its own blood while lost in self-love; and can revel with him in the pure rapture of knowing God!

It need not have taken Joseph thirteen years to get where God wanted him to be. The archers "sorely grieved him, and shot at him, and hated him" only while self was alive to be hurt by them. God was waiting all the while to shower upon him "the blessings of Heaven above, blessings of the deep that lieth under," blessings that should prevail "to the utmost bound of the everlasting hills." So, too, is He waiting for you. Almighty Love can only keep you from the deadly arrows of your three mortal foes—the world, the flesh, and the Devil—so far as your life is "hid with Christ in God." But if you retreat from them to that blessed hiding place, it can and will keep you. God is waiting now to

make you forget—forget all that separates you from Him,
all that is sin-stained, and self-stained, all that you should
wish to remember no more. He will take your sins and cast
them behind His back, to be remembered against you no
more for ever. He will "take your memory" and make it
dwell only upon His glorious words and workings.

And you—how long, by an imperfect consecration, a
waning faith, will you keep Him waiting?

God Overruling

So now it was not you that sent me hither, but God
(Gen. 45:8).

Three times over, Joseph told his brothers that God sent
him down into Egypt; that they had not done it, although
he admits, "Ye sold me hither."

Joseph had the keen, spiritual vision, which comes from
much practice in looking to God, and considering His
works and ways. He had the pure heart which "sees God"
in all its circumstances. He had the eye of faith. Unbelief
sees only unfinished, unmeaning parts of life; faith sees a
harmonious, happy whole, even before the pattern is finished on the loom of time.

Comrade, with what sort of eyes do you look out upon
life? Does God manage your life, through your perfect
yielding and trust in Him? or do you still feel the heavy
hand of "fate,"; and "fortune" upon you, as in the days
when you were an unbelieving sinner? Did God send you to
your hard Corps, or is Head-quarters solely responsible for
your being there? I verily believe my Superior Officers to be
guided by God; but, none the less, I should tremble for fear

of possible mistakes if I were not so wholly in His hand myself that neither saint nor sinner can touch or influence my life except by His direction. In that fact lies comfort, peace of mind, a settled tranquillity.

I remember hearing my mother remonstrate with a Methodist minister who had been given the poorest appointment in his Conference.

"I would not go," she said, decidedly. "With your family they ought not to send you to such a place. Why don't you object, and tell the presiding elder that you cannot go, and you will not?"

I remember, too, the satisfied smile that broke out on the minister's face. "I have never said a word about my appointment to anyone by God," he told her. "He sends me about, and He must want me to go to Margaretville. Somebody must go there, and why not I? But I put the matter always in God's Hands, and I know that He settles it."

At that time I did not understand Holiness, and it amazed me that this man should be content with poverty and hardship, just because he thought them God's will for him, while others in the Conference—his inferiors in spirituality, scholarship, and natural force—had excellent appointments. But now, I understand. God was his portion, his inheritance, his home, his present good, his future expectation, just as He was to Abraham, to Joseph, and the long line of His own, since their day. Is He that to you?

He Careth

And the Lord said, I have surely seen the affliction of My people which are in Egypt, and have heard their cry by reason of their taskmasters; for I know their

> *sorrows; and I am come down to deliver them out of*
> *the hand of the Egyptians, and to bring them up out*
> *of that land unto a good land and a large, unto a land*
> *flowing with milk and honey* (Ex. 3:7, 8).

The Devil would often have us believe that God has forgotten us or that His mind is so taken up with the great affairs of His universe that He cannot stoop to such trifles as our griefs and pains. But when God tells us that His care goes down far past our immortal souls, to look after the winged mites of the air, we are bound to believe that it takes in the intermediate things of our human lives.

Believe it! Why, God has guarded our faith at this very point, and expressly told us that He looks after our daily doings! Men of faith know this, and have always known it. "Thou numberest my steps," cried Job. "The steps of a good man are ordered by the Lord," declared David. And the feet of these two surely trod some briery ways! But amid the thorns God led their feet. He counted each step, measuring their number against the faith appropriated grace, to see that not one step too far was taken. "Thou lookest narrowly unto all my paths." "Doth not he see my ways, and count all my steps."

A girl who had endured great opposition as a Slum Soldier both at and away from home, and who had the grace to wear the only uniform in a great city, against the will and tongues of mother, pastor, and people, had yet to be turned out of doors late at night, in a strange city, to find shelter where she could, before she realized that God cared about the details of her life! But, somehow, the homeless feel of the hard stones under her feet, and the chill of the wintry night air striking through her, drove her to God with such wide-open eyes of despair, that she saw that He cared. She felt in her heart that He knew her sorrow, and had made it His.

Then, He put it into her heart to go to the right place to

find a home; and when she walked into its friendly door, she carried with her, hid in her heart, not any longer a Master, but a Father, a Brother, a Friend, a Lover, who knew perfectly well what had been said and done to her, and cared that she had been scorned and cast out for His sake. "I never used to think that God cared about trifles," she said, "but I know better now."

But where had her eyes been all those years, when reading His word? He afflicts the children of men, though "not willingly." "Whom the Lord loveth He chasteneth." "For Thou, Lord, has proved us," says the Psalmist, in a great song of praise; "Thou hast tried us as silver is tried." That means a hot trial; a thorough searching out of everything impure. The last atom of silver has to feel the purifying fire, and the last little feeling of yours which is contrary to your own good, and therefore, to your own happiness, cannot be suffered to escape. "Thou broughtest us into the net," sings grateful faith adoringly. "Thou laidst affliction upon our loins. Thou hast caused men to rise over our heads; we went through fire and through water, but Thou broughtest us out into a wealthy place." That is the end and object of all God's dealings with us—to bring us "out into a wealthy place."

And that the only way into this large and fair land is through floods or flames is because of our blindness, obstinacy, stiffness of neck, and hardness of heart towards God. We will not believe. Jesus Himself says, "Ye will not come unto Me that ye might have life." This lassie who had gone so far on the way to Heaven, serving God uninterruptedly through seven years of trial, had to be turned into the streets to find out that God cared for her with a tender, personal all-embracing love! It needed the affliction of loneliness and strangerhood to explain to her what her Bible had always declared plainly and openly—that He loved her with an everlasting love.

God sends us out of our homes, and out of our native

land, to learn what we will not learn by our own fire-sides—to know God, and to know Him as Love, and Love alone. When prosperity sheds its sunlight over us, we bask in its heat and light, and think little of God. And so, since the knowledge of Him is our only happiness, our only good, He sends darkness, and blight, and loss, and crashing storm, that we may fly to find Him.

The Israelites would never have left their well-fed slavery, despite its dangers to soul and body, if they could have had a good time in it. So God made their burdens heavy and rigorous to drive them out into His grand, man-making freedom. He knew their sorrows, for He had appointed them as the only way by which to bring them to true joy in serving Him. He knows your sorrows, and He grieves over the necessity of laying them upon you, or, as in the case of Job, He allows them for the sake of blessing others. "Oh that My people had hearkened unto Me, and Israel had walked in My ways! I should soon have subdued their enemies, and turned My hand against their adversaries. . . . He should have fed them also with the finest of the wheat: and with honey out of the rock should I have satisfied thee!"

God has made all the pleasant and lovely things of earth for His children. Why is it, then, that *you* are shut out from your birthright in them? Because you cannot be trusted with it; you have not enough obedience and faith to prove yourself worthy. You would wrest God's gifts to your own destruction, and He loves you too well to let you do it. He means to save you, to sanctify you, to glorify you, if patient, long-suffering, infinite love can do it.

> Among so many, can He care?
> Can special love be everywhere?
> A myriad homes—a myriad ways—
> And God's eyes over every place?

I asked; my soul bethought of this:
In just that very place of His
Where He has put and keepeth you,
God hath no other thing to do!

Wanted! Speaking Trumpets

*And Moses said unto the Lord, O my Lord, I am not
eloquent, neither heretofore, nor since Thou hast
spoken unto Thy servant: but I am slow of speech,
and of a slow tongue. And the Lord said unto him,
Who hath made man's mouth? or who maketh the
dumb, or deaf, or the seeing, or the blind? have not I
the Lord? Now therefore go and I will be with thy
mouth, and teach thee what thou shalt say. And he
said, O my Lord, send, I pray Thee, by the hand of
him whom Thou wilt send* (Ex. 4:10-13).

Moses has many sympathizers among Christians in his
reluctance to take up the part of a public pleader for God.
Most of us are "slow of speech," and even the grace of God
does not provide us with silver tongues and a winning
speech. We prefer the retirement of our homes to a public
platform. We would be glad to serve God secretly, and pray
for sinners, instead of preaching to them. We would fain
keep out of print, and sink for ever out of the general memory.

But Moses forgot—God help us to remember!—that "it
is not by might or by power," but by God's Spirit that His
work is done. It must be that Moses lost something in so
shunning the shame of the Cross that could never be made
good to him while he sheltered behind Aaron's better pow-

ers of speech. God had not demanded eloquence of him, or that he should dazzle or argue Pharaoh into consenting to His will; He needed him simply as a messenger. God wanted a common speaking trumpet, and Moses declined to be anything but a first-class silver cornet.

"Who hath made man's mouth?" Who so likely to know whether or not we are fit for messengers, as He who created us? You are not eloquent? Neither was Paul. "For though I be rude in speech," he says (Rotherham's translation: "uncultured in my discourse") "yet not in knowledge." Paul had a knowledge of Jesus as his personal Savior, and so he passed that knowledge on to his fellow men in the spirit and power of Jesus; the manner and style of doing it did not matter to him. And again he writes: "For his letters, say they, are weighty and powerful, but his bodily presence is weak, and his speech contemptible." But Paul did not give over carrying his message because of these unpleasant facts, although he was very conscious of them. He tells us, "There was given to me a thorn in the flesh, the messenger of Satan to buffet me. . . . For this thing I besought the Lord thrice, that it might depart from me; and He said unto me, My grace is sufficient for thee: for My strength is made perfect in weakness. Most gladly therefore will I rather glory in my infirmities, that the power of Christ may rest upon me!" He had trodden the way of death to self, and Jesus Christ had full possession of his poor body.

Can you imagine Paul thinking about the impression he made on an audience, or caring what the people thought of his looks, his eloquence, his personality? No; but he cared very much what the audience thought of his Master, and, "base in outward appearance" (2 Cor. 10:1, margin) as he was, he made them think of Him; made them feel and know that His Spirit possesses His servant's body; and so he laid broad and deep the foundations of the Church of God. Go out in the spirit of Paul, and God will use you for the purpose for which He has called you.

Again, some people plead lack of education as an excuse for not answering the call of God to carry His message of Salvation. "If eloquence is not a necessity, at least a good stock of words, and knowledge of their right use, is needful," they say.

"The world did not get to know God by its wisdom" (1 Cor. 1:21, Rotherham); and Paul declares in the same chapter where he tells us this, that Christ sent him to preach the Gospel "not with wisdom of words." Why?—"lest thereby the Cross of Christ should be made of no account."

And again he says, "I was with you in weakness, and in fear, and in much trembling. And my speech and my preaching was not with enticing words of man's wisdom, but in demonstration of the Spirit, and of power." Paul was evidently much lacking in the outer graces which attract men's eyes, and in the peculiar gifts of a natural orator. Yet the world feels increasingly to this day the power—not born with him, but given by God—with which he carried God's message.

Paul took what Moses did not—the promise,"I will be with thy mouth, and teach thee what thou shalt say." And you—what more do you need? Are not His presence and His teaching a strong enough warrant that if you undertake to carry messages in His name and strength, His end will be accomplished, and He will be well pleased with you?

"Now, therefore, go!"

The Hardened Heart

And the Lord hardened the heart of Pharaoh, and he hearkened not unto them (Ex. 9:12).

Children always seem puzzled to know why Pharaoh was considered responsible for his wrongdoing, and punished for it, when God hardened his heart. Only the other day, one was asking me, "But how was he naughty? He could not help himself, if God made his heart hard."

God hardened Pharaoh's heart only by withdrawing His presence; and Pharaoh was directly responsible for that withdrawing, because he grieved away the Holy Spirit by his persistent disobedience and rebellion.

Look back to the account of the first plague, and see how be began the hardening process. Moses had told him what God demanded, and performed a great marvel of God's power before him; but Pharaoh "turned and went into his house, neither did he set his heart to this also."

Just what sinners do nowadays. They listen to God's warning, look at the miracles of His converting power wrought before their eyes, and go back to their homes to eat and drink and sin, careless alike of His love and His judgments. They do not set their hearts to consider the truth; they prefer lies; they harden their hearts with them.

After the second plague, Pharaoh hardened his own heart; he resisted God more openly. It took more of an effort this time, for some impression had been made upon him by his trouble, so that he asked for relief. But he was only sorry for the consequences of his sin, not for the sin itself, and the moment the hand of chastisement was lightened from upon him he said, "No!" to God again.

That's exactly what the children of Israel did later on. Zechariah says, "They made their hearts as an adamant stone, lest they should hear the law, and the word which the Lord of Hosts hath sent in His Spirit by the former prophets."

And after Pharaoh or the Jews, or you, have driven away the Holy Spirit by too-long rebellion, God's gracious presence will have withdrawn, and the sinning heart be hopelessly hardened. But only in that sense is God the Author of this work.

The Kindness of God

That thou mayest know (Ex. 9:14).

God had only one object in view in His dealings with Pharaoh as an individual, and that was, to bring him to a personal knowledge—a saving knowledge, if he would only have it—of the Lord. It is true that when Pharaoh put himself in the way of God's purpose for the Hebrews he made trouble and suffering for himself, but God had only peace in His heart and mind towards Pharaoh. He was as truly love for that poor, proud Egyptian as for any soul of our own time and country.

But how about that verse where He says, "And in very deed for this cause have I raised thee up, for to show in thee My power, and that My name may be declared throughout all the earth"?

God had raised Pharaoh up from his sick bed (verses 10, 11) to give him another chance to repent. Pharaoh might have become converted to God then, if he only would, and have shown forth the power of God far more mightily through his conversion than through the penalties incurred by his stubbornness, and through the awful death to which his sin brought him. God meant Pharaoh to become His servant and follower, declaring His power to save through all the earth, as a mighty king could do. He meant him to know the joy of sins forgiven, the river-like peace of harmony with God, the wonderful beauty of life as a child of the Most High; and to this end He healed him, and gave him another chance.

The ten plagues might better be called the ten opportunities. Each one opened a door to Pharaoh through which he might enter and be reconciled to God; each one sounded a clarion warning to him to repent; each one showed the

37

clinging, long-suffering, patient love of God, that could not bear to destroy His creature while there was any hope that he might be saved.

"As I live, saith the Lord God, I have no pleasure in the death of the wicked; but that the wicked turn from his way and live; turn ye, turn ye from your evil ways, for why will ye die?"

God is love. His word says it, and all His works declare it. But that love is much misrepresented by the sentimental preaching which takes out of it both truth and justice, and makes it save the sinner in his sins. Salvation is not a bare escape from Hell; it is an escape from present sin. God's love called loudly to Pharaoh many times, and would have delivered him, up to the very borders of the engulfing sea; but he hated goodness, and hated God. So does every sinner; and unless they meet the love of God by repentance and faith, the fate of Pharaoh's soul must be theirs.

Worldly Companions

And a mixed multitude went up also with them (Ex. 12:38).

More and more, people are coming to draw lessons for the individual from the history of nations, and this mixed multitude teaches a marked one for young Converts just leaving the land of darkness. For they "fell a lusting" not very long after they had set out; they were not satisfied with the things God provided for them, but went longing and seeking after the things of the world, and tempted the children of Israel to follow them in their sin.

Cut loose from worldly companions, once for all, when God has converted you! There are always hangers-on about every Army Corps, who will not yield their hearts to God, who never mean to, and yet they like the society of God's people, and seek them out in preference to sinners. They appear to have a refined moral taste and to like a faint flavor of spirituality in their friends; they like people, too, whom they can trust in their talk and action.

But if you admit them to fellowship with you in all outward things, and put them on the same footing with God's people in your friendship and association, they will cause your downfall in spiritual things, just as these outsiders did that of the children of Israel; and your soul, like theirs, will fall under a blighting plague.

The Hebrews, being set to live by bread from Heaven, ought not to have listened to continual talk about cucumbers and melons, leeks and potherbs; it could only stir up gluttony and discontent in them. Listening to it was like the looking back of Lot's wife. You, being set to feed your soul on heavenly manna, ought not to listen to the old talk of worldly trifles on which your starving soul fed when you were a sinner.

Your mind is to be "set on things above"; why drag it down to discuss things below—gossip, fashions, amusements, and newspaper horrors, which cannot profit, and ought not to interest it? You are living for the next world, and have given up this world by a solemn vow, as well as by the converting grace of God. What have you to do, in the way of friendship and intimacy, with worldliness? Cut loose from them, before they draw you into sin! But how? Talk your new language to them incessantly; plead with them earnestly, ardently for their Salvation; pray with them; read the Bible to them, and soon they will either be converted or will leave you and drift away back into Egypt.

Prayer, Believing and Otherwise

And when Pharaoh drew nigh, the children of Israel lifted up their eyes, and, behold, the Egyptians marched after them; and they were sore afraid: and the children of Israel cried out unto the Lord (Ex. 14:10).

"Crying unto the Lord" is just what Moses did a little later (verse 15); but Oh! the difference between the prayer of these faithless Israelites and that of the trusting man of God!

The Israelites stopped praying to revile Moses. They asked God to deliver them from the Egyptians, and yet declared that they would die in the wilderness! These are two striking characteristics of unbelieving prayer; unbelief expects nothing from God, even when it asks of Him; and all its praying makes no difference with its after-life.

But faith expects something. Before he got orders from God to go forward, Moses told his frightened followers that God would save them, and that their dreaded enemies should be seen no more for ever. And once he had finished praying, he put his faith into action, stretched his shepherd's rod out over the wide waters, and walked on, expecting them, too, to obey God.

I knew a woman who for nine long years cried to God to reveal Himself to her. She had no God, and a Savior seemed to her the most desirable thing in life. But all her passionate calling was in vain; there was no faith in her! She did not expect any answer; she only expressed her misery in her crying. God will answer repentance; He must always answer faith; but what can He have to say to unbelief?

Another woman has been trying for many years to be sanctified by God; she has gone out to altars and Penitent-Forms; she has devoured all the Holiness literature she could lay hands on; she has talked, meditated, prayed; in short, she had done everything, except believe!

"But how is it possible," do you ask, "for an agnostic, like the first woman, to believe? She has not word of God to accept, for she does not consider the Bible as the word of God." I answer: "Let her put the alleged word of God to the test. Let her take, for instance, the promise, "Ye shall seek Me, and find Me, when ye shall search for Me with all your heart," and fulfil the conditions, and see if she does not find the promise fulfilled in her own experience. She will know that there is a God, and she will go on to know Him as a personal, loving, forgiving, keeping Savior. I have known this done by an infidel with glorious success."

And how shall a Christian believe for Sanctification who has tried so long and failed? Ah, that is a sorry question! If, in all her Christian experience of so many years, she has not found her God to be a God of truth, a God of love, who is more willing to give us the Holy Spirit than we are to give good gifts to our children; who gives the Spirit "without measure"; who is able to keep the souls committed to Him; able to keep His oath, that we should walk in Holiness and true righteousness before Him all the days of our life; then it is hard to see how such an unhappy soul could believe. But will any Christian dare to say that?

Stop crying out, poor soul, and take the forward steps of faith. Believe God!

> Because I spent the strength Thou gavest me
>   In struggle which Thou never didst ordain,
> And have but dregs of life to offer Thee,
>   O God, I do repent!

No Excuse for Murmuring

And the whole congregation of the children of Israel murmured against Moses and Aaron in the wilderness. . . . And Moses and Aaron said unto all the children of Israel, . . . He heareth your murmurings against the Lord; and what are we, that ye murmur against us (Ex. 16:2, 6, 7)?

If any persons ever had an excuse for complaining, it really seems as if these poor Hebrews had one now. Out there in the desert, with nothing edible growing, no game within reach, no opportunity to work for food, no place in which to buy any, with children and dumb animals clamoring for it—was not this a hard pinch for them?

Put yourself mentally in their place; realize the trial to heart, body, and faith; and then compare these things with your own actual situation. Would it be easier for you to bear life and trust God in that Sinaitic desert than in London, in Castleacre, in some little Yorkshire hamlet, or wherever you are now?

Not one bit. You would probably have groaned and complained at Moses with the loudest of them; and maybe, when the trial of thirst came on you afterwards, you would have actually thrown a stone at him, instead of being "ready to," as the impatient Jews were.

But had they, hard as these things were to bear, any excuse for murmuring and complaining about them? No, none—absolutely none. God in His word allows none, and reason and justice are against it, when we come to think about.

God brought them into this place and arranged these circumstances, with the full play of infinite wisdom and love. These things were meant to work out not only their spiritual profit, but, through that, their temporal good.

They were meant to throw them wholly, with a fearless, aggressive faith, on God; and so, to put them in possession of all His wide, magnificent promises for the life that now is, as well as for that which is to come. They would have lacked "no good thing"; they would have "inherited the earth"; they would have "abundantly satisfied with His goodness."

The way out of all their troubles was to pray, as individuals, and as a people; to take the Throne of God by storm with their believing prayers; to ask and receive. But they preferred to scold Moses! Tremendous anti-climax, is it not? But it is a pitiful and shameful one as well, a sorrowful and a mournful one. God sends the gracious angels of trouble and trial upon His people to draw them nearer to Him, to cut them off from human help and comfort, to make them so call out to Him in faith that He can bless them as He never has done before. But they turn away from this open door of love and blessing and begin a foolish and wicked murmuring against Him! They shut the door of hope against themselves, and open one of doubt, gloom, despair, backsliding. Was there any excuse for the stubborn Jews? Is there any for you?

Complaining brings its own curse with it, besides incurring the wrath of God. "Jealousy is cruel as the grave," said the wise man; but grumbling is as bitter and painful as a wasting, mortal sickness. It is a canker—corroding, wasting, agonizing; it is contrary to health of soul and body. "Do all things without murmuring and disputing," commanded God through Paul.

What is the cure? How shall one get rid of the habit, or ward off its approaches?

There is a systematic course of exercises laid down by David in the 105th Psalm, which, if regularly and persistently carried out, will cure and keep in peace and joy any complainer. "Give thanks unto the Lord." Take stock of your past and present blessings, and be grateful for them.

I knew a mother who, while her baby lay scarlet and burning with fever, was tempted to repine about it. But there was the fever—lamentations would not cure it. So she began to thank God that she had a cool room for her darling, a plentiful supply of linen, a fair knowledge of nursing, some one to send for the doctor, disinfectants to keep the other little one safe, and, most of all, the Salvation of God for her comfort and stay. As she counted up these things, she saw that nothing was lacking, that the Lord had just heaped up gifts and benefits upon her, and she poured out praises and thanks till the Devil fled away, and the sun seemed to have risen in the darkness of that sick room. If we give thanks in proportion to all God's gifts to our souls as well as bodies, we shall never have any time for complaining.

"Call upon His name." Tell Him your needs and wishes, and ask Him to conform your will in your circumstances wholly to His; ask Him to let you find the blessing and the glory He has hidden away in the surrounding clouds for you, and to enrich your soul as fully as He has meant to do.

"Sing unto Him." A hymn in the heart, even if one cannot sing out for fear of disturbing someone, is a great help. Jesus sang a hymn just before He went out to the Mount of Olives for the last time, and who knows how the psalm of praise may have strengthened His burdened heart for that hour of consummate anguish? We sing praises to God when the flesh fails and the spirit is almost sinking, and with the song comes the strengthening joy of the Spirit into our weary souls.

"Glory ye in His holy name." Exult in your God, and you thereby triumph over all your foes; you lose sight of earth; you are already a crowned victor.

"Let the heart of them rejoice that seek the Lord." You cannot help being happy when you have got as far as this, if your heart has been faithfully exercised in all the preceding commands; you will go on to "seek the Lord and His strength" exultingly; you will have forgotten that you had anything to complain about by this time. You will "remember His marvellous works that He hath done," to the exclusion of any unpleasant and mean things that some one else may have done; and, when you meet your family or friends, you will be able to finish out the prescription—"to make known his deeds among the people," and "talk of all His wondrous works."

On Eagles' Wings

I bare you on eagles' wings, and brought you unto Myself (Ex. 19:4).

It is not only to pardon, peace, and purity, that God means to bring His people, but to such an intimate knowledge of Himself as results in a perfect union of their being with His. The subject is one for volumes, not pages, and has been made clear and plain by many writers who have advanced in spiritual growth to this—notably, John Fletcher and his wife, Thomas Upham, Madame Guyon, and Fenelon. In these days of libraries, almost anyone can get at these human teachers; but without any earthly help, God by His Spirit will bring into heavenly union with Himself the soul which desires Him as its sole good. He gives us rich gifts, but they are not to be the objects of our love. His desire is to bring us to Himself, as the personal Possessor of all our being.

God's side of this perfect union is expressed in His word: "Thy Maker is thy Husband"; "I have loved thee with an everlasting love"; "I am married unto you"; while that of His people is no less clearly set forth in the Psalms and major prophets.

But people of these days who can recognize, line by line, their own experience in the following verses of Madame Guyon, know what it is to be brought by God "to Himself":

> To me, 'tis equal, whether love ordain
>   My life or death, appoint me pain or ease;
> My soul perceives no real ill in pain,
>   In ease or health no real good she sees.
>
> One good she covets, and that good alone,
>   To choose Thy will, from selfish bias free;
> And to prefer a cottage to a throne,
>   And grief to comfort, if it pleases Thee.
>
> My country, Lord, art Thou alone,
> No other can I claim or own;
> The point where all my wishes meet,
> My law, my love; life's only sweet.
>
> I hold by nothing here below;
> Appoint my journey, and I go;
> Though pierced by scorn, opprest by pride,
> I feel the good—feel naught beside.
>
> No frowns of men can hurtful prove
> To souls on fire with heavenly love;
> Though men and devils both condemn,
> No gloomy days arise from them.

"I Have Heard"

Thou shalt not raise" [margin, "receive"] "a false report" (Ex. 23:1).

Did you ever hear a story about some one else prefaced by the words, "I have heard, but I do not know how true it is," that was other than damaging to its subject? I never did, and it seems to me that this is the sort of talk which God's strong "Thou shalt not" is meant to kill.

As a speaker, we should never repeat any alleged facts about another for the truth of which we are not prepared to vouch. As listener, one should decline to hear—"receive"—such tales, and, with love and meekness, should point out the breach of law to the offender. There are many Christians who repeat chance tales about others, never dreaming that they are breaking a law of God in doing it. Let the light of the word shine on them through you. So will you both help a soul and carry out another command in this same chapter—to "keep thee far from a false matter."

"I Will Guide Thee"

Behold, I send an angel before thee, to keep thee in the way. . . . Beware of him, and obey his voice (Ex. 23: 20, 21).

"Mamma," said my small boy the other day, "I'm sure that Jesus talks to me. I hear His voice in my heart, and it tells me when I do right, and when I don't do right. But I

47

can't always hear it." A serious pause. "When I play too hard, and when I talk too much, I can't hear the voice!"

Is not that your case sometimes?

When two ways open before you, and your heart inclines to one of them, and fears come up lest God should mean the other for you, do not rush off to some friend for counsel—do not talk the matter over and over, and bring up reasons why the pleasant path must be the right one—be silent, and let God's voice be heard. Quiet the tumult of your nature, "Let all the earth" about you "be silent before Him," and listen. If you wish, in your inmost soul, to know God's will for you, He will surely reveal it when you will let him.

Mixed Worship

And they rose up early on the morrow, and offered burnt offerings, and brought peace offerings: and the people sat down to eat and to drink, and rose up to play (Ex. 32:6).

In every part of the Christian world one can see this curious travesty of religion performed daily. People going promptly and regularly through their fixed ceremonial of worship, and spending the rest of the day or week, as the case may be, in self-gratification and amusement. If you inquire as to the object of their apparent devotion, you will find it a god of their own making—it may be a creed, a building, a society, a ritual; it is not the living Jehovah.

The pure worship of God takes out of a man all desire for worldly things. He will no more spend his time outside of Meetings in sensuous indulgence and idle amusement than he will pass it in downright wickedness. He cannot. His thoughts and wishes are continually upon God and His work; his time and strength are not his own, but God's; his pleasure is in communing with God in secret, or rejoicing in Him with His people; his recreation, even, is in things which do not separate his mind wholly from its supreme object.

The practical application of our text is this: if you find in yourself habits of eating, drinking, and amusement, or even desires of them, which are not for the glory of God, this is a danger signal. Prove yourself before God, and see whether your love for Him is pure and free from all admixture of worldly desire and fleshly longings; whether your experience is as well defined and clear as it once was; whether God is really first in your inmost thought, feeling and purpose.

Old habits may have been kept up thoughtlessly, new ones crept in unconsciously; but test them by the word of God, by the spirit of that word, and see if they bear the stamp and seal of a whole-hearted desire for the glory of God. Consider whether your amusements are such as to promote the Kingdom of God ("righteousness, peace, and joy in the Holy Ghost") in your own heart, and, by your example, in the hearts of others. If not, for the love of God and your own soul, drop them, and get all desire for them taken out of your heart. "Faithful is He who has called you, who also will do it."

Separated

Wherein shall it be known here that I and Thy people have found grace in Thy sight? is it not in that Thou goest with us? so shall we be separated, I and Thy

*people, from all the people that are upon the face of
the earth* (Ex.33:16).

There is an eternal line drawn between the true children
of God and the people of the world, making a difference as
unmistakable as that between daylight and darkness, as
great as that between good and evil. In fact, it *is* the difference between good and evil. The children of God have been
made like Him, and He goes with them on their ordered
way; the children of the world have willed to follow the
Devil, and they, in spirit, are like their chosen master.

The fact that God goes with an individual necessarily
separates him from the people of the world. Invert this
proposition, and you have the truth that lack of separation
between the world and a man proves that God is not with
him. He may have longings for God and goodness, high
aspirations, excellent desires; but he will find that these
avail him nothing for Salvation—he must have the abiding
presence of God; and Moses found, and all saints have
found, that this presence separates them "from all people
that are upon the face of the earth."

Do men, angels, and devils know on which side of the
line you stand?

Break the Images

*Take heed to thyself, lest thou make a covenant with
the inhabitants of the land whither thou goest, lest it
be for a snare in the midst of thee: but ye shall
destroy their altars, break their images, and cut down
their groves* (Ex. 34:12, 13).

The law of God, written in the hearts of His sanctified people, has become a part of their inmost being, and it works out in their conduct as naturally as their physical life does in the exercise of the different parts of the body. It is not difficult for a healthy eye to show us pictures of our surroundings; not unpleasant for a healthy ear to report to us the sounds of nature; nor is it either hard or distasteful for a healthy soul to carry out the whole will of God, to match every detail of conduct to His perfect law. Difficulty and pain do not attend natural workings; they indicate an unhealthy or diseased state.

If God's law seems hard and unnecessarily strict, it proves that the soul is out of order; that the heart needs a fresh application of the Cleansing Blood. Get to your knees, comrade, and find out the Physician with His balm.

A wealthy woman in New England lived "like other people;" built a big house for show, furnished it luxuriously, dressed herself to adorn it, and set a table calculated to impress people with the size of her bank account. All this she did in ignorance of God; but by and by He saved and sanctified her. Then, the big house seemed like a prison, its unnecessary furnishings became multiplied reproaches, and she wanted to sell the place, build a little cottage not too good for the servant of a Carpenter to live in, and order her whole way of dressing and living on a humble, unobtrusive scale. There was no Salvation Army in the place to influence or shape her ideas, and she did not consult any religious people about changing her mode of life. She had stopped worshiping mammon, and the law of God in the center of all her desires, made her long to "break her images." A new sense of beauty sprang up within her which needed neither sculpture nor painting to satisfy it, but found scope for its exercise in the spiritual and moral realm, while God's works in nature fully met all need in what remained of her old artistic perception.

There was no idea of self-sacrifice in her wish to give up the old home; it was simply that she was no longer of the world, and pretentiousness of living, like any other form of worldliness, cramped her free spirit. She did not wish her surroundings to revive those former worldly thoughts, feelings, and associations which had once been, and must still be, fatal to her spiritual life.

Hers is no solitary instance. I have known many who after sanctification have striven to make their exterior lives as different as the interior. They no longer attend concerts, not because they cannot any more appreciate grand and intricate harmonies, nor be moved by them, but because music dissociated from the praise of God leaves them unsatisfied.

"If any man be in Christ Jesus . . . old things are passed away." Not only the old sins, but the old delights. The craving soul has found what satisfies it, and it demands of ears, tongue, and brain that they shall minister to it of the things of God. It sees beauty in nature multiplied a thousandfold, but art loses its charm. Sounds that do not suggest Jesus please no longer; sounds that make Him plainer to their perception fascinate and draw, even though the cultivated ear may deem them discords. Ideas that do not circle about Him have no power to stir or hold. God manifest in Christ Jesus appears the sole object worthy of study and meditation, and the very thought of Him is recreation and rest.

And does not the great law of continuity demand this? Would God design us to love the things of the world as such all through our allotted space of time, and then, uneducated, unprepared, to enter an eternity where these things are non-existent? He does not. His laws are consistent, practical, perfect. Himself is Heaven, and He converts us from any love of these "old things" to a love of the new, satisfying things "in Christ Jesus." He gives us a heaven

here from which His laws, if lived out, will take us into the
unknown Heaven hereafter without a break or jar.

Don't you see, comrade, that when you have come so far
in thought as to God's Heaven that the world's images" are
out of sight, out of mind, almost out of comprehension?
One comes back to them with a sort of mental shock!

Are there any images left in the range of your being? If
so, in the name of Jehovah, break them! If the secret taber-
nacle of the Most High, with its perpetual and adorable
Sacrifice made for you, its songs in the heart, its odorous
incense of perpetual prayer, its daily voices and miracles in
your own life, do not satisfy your nature, will the old
"images" do it?

Willing Offerings

*Take ye from among you an offering unto the Lord;
whosoever is of a willing heart, let him bring it, an
offering of the Lord* (Ex. 35:5).

But suppose the heart is not willing! Does that free one
from making the offering? "The Lord loveth a cheerful
giver." But suppose there is no cheerfulness about it,
although we know that the gift ought to be made?

The willingness is an essential, so if it be lacking, we
should go to our Father and get the lack supplied, just as we
would any other.

Our hearts are of more importance than our gifts; and
the gift-giving is only an evidence of the state of our heart.
Any unwillingness to give, when we ought to do so, shows
a heart unlike that of our God, who has given us not only

all we possess, but gave His very throne and Godhood for us, in giving us the gift of His humanity.

How a holy heart delights in giving! It has received so much that its treasures overflow. It pours its possessions out on the needy like water, and keeps a bare living for itself. A Methodist minister, living near the Canadian border, was sanctified by God a few years ago, and preached Salvation till his dead church rose as one man against him. They cut his salary down to less than one-third of the stipulated figure, and then, for nearly four months, paid him nothing at all. His little adopted baby was in need of clothes, which he was unable to buy, till extra persecution on the part of his official board raised the sympathy of outsiders, who gave him some money.

Just at that time, two Army specials came to the town, and out of the abundance of his few dollars this poor saint must needs entertain them! He kept them over the Sabbath, and when, on Monday, they opened the lunch with which he had set them on their journey, there was an envelope in the little parcel holding a dollar! Surely the angels must have seen a halo about that soiled green bill!

But suppose you or I had been in the minister's place, would not little Tom's thin shoes, and Eleanor's patched pinafore, and the wife's shabby dress, and the apology for a carpet, and what not besides, have stood up in our minds and clamored for that dollar? They all might, and yet the dollar should go willingly. So marvelous a thing is God's grace; it works such wonders, and moves such mountains, in common-place, ordinary little hearts like yours and mine!

You give—perhaps beyond your means and more than your friends do—but do you give in the name of Jesus, and with a willing heart? If not, God will make you willing, if you ask Him. Hallelujah!

Dependence on God

*And He hath filled him with the Spirit of God, in
wisdom, in understanding, and in knowledge, and in
all manner of workmanship: and to devise curious
works, to work in gold, and in silver, and in brass,
and in the cutting of stones, to set them, and in
carving of wood, to make any manner of cunning
work. And he hath put in his heart that he may teach*
(Ex. 35:31-34).

Here is a big drop of comfort for the people who do what
is called "behind-the-scenes" work—for those who make
uniforms and trim bonnets, sell the books, prepare the soup
and ladle it out, set up type, run The Army laundries, bak-
eries, and knitting machines. It shows that God as distinctly endues them with His Spirit to do such work for Him, as
He does others to fill the priestly offices. Bless the dear
Lord for ever!

There is no reason to conclude that these two men
whom God called to plan and build for Him had natural
aptitude as architects and designers; the Holy Spirit could
supply their natural lack in brain and ability. So He can and
will for us. Many of us have proved it; some of us ought to
have proved it, but we have chosen instead to fail.

But to appropriate God's power to do everyday hand and
head work for Him, we need to seek His face continually,
humbly, fervently. If "he that trusteth in his own heart is a
fool," much more is he that trusts in his own intellect, or
sense, to do God's work acceptably, independent of His
Spirit!

Talebearing

Thou shalt not go up and down as a talebearer among thy people (Lev. 19:16).

There are two kinds of talebearing—the malicious, intentionally wicked sort, and recognized by every one as evil, and another chatty, newsy, comparatively innocent species, resulting rather from a lack of earnest intention to do good then from the will to do wrong. Both kinds come under the ban of this immortal law of peace.

I knew a lassie who loved God and souls, but who had a keen eye for anything wrong, and when she espied something not as it should be, would take the trouble so to her heart that it marred the peace of her face, and she would go about with knit brows and darkened eyes seeking someone to whom she could tell her sorrow. Now it was not enough that her motive was not a wicked one; it should have been positively good, and then she should only have told of the wrong in order to get it righted.

By her conduct she unintentionally made mischief and trouble, and unconsciously sowed the seeds of discord in more than one Army Corps. At last she mentioned a lamentable case of hypocrisy and double-dealing to an Officer in the presence of two Soldiers.

"Do you know that story to be true?" asked her listener.

"N—no," hesitated Maggie, "only the folks all said so. It was told to me for true, and I thought it such a pity for a Soldier to be going on like that!"

"But you don't know it for a fact," said the Officer, sticking to the main point, "and you have told it to three of us, strangers to the man, who cannot possible help him. You have injured his reputation with us, who are his comrades, even if we don't know him, so that if we happen to hear his name after this we must couple it with "hypocrite"! Is that the way the Bible teaches us to do?

Maggie, an old Soldier, had never thought of it before in that light! But her words of confession, and her humble, childlike prayer about it showed that the late-discovered law of God had found a quick home in her heart.

The Duty of Rebuking

Thou shalt in any wise rebuke thy neighbor, and not suffer sin upon him (Lev.19:17).

This is by no means an easy thing to do. It is often very hard, as most of us have found.

Sometime ago two girls were passing criticisms upon comrades in my hearing. To the simple question, "Have you dealt with this comrade about her soul?" they returned two most astonishing answers. One said, "Certainly not. She is my Superior Officer. It is not my place to deal with the Staff about their souls!" The other said, "No, it is her Major's place to look after her soul. I might report the case, since I have discovered it, but that is all."

But Almighty God recognizes no distinction between Commissioner and Candidate, between bishop and layman, in His universal law. He lumps us all together as "neighbors," nothing more, and certainly nothing less. Our General, the Pope and all his train, take rank there with paupers and criminals and the saints of today. It is a sort of judgment day word, bringing all humanity down to its true place under the eye of God. The man or woman whose deeds or words God brings to your knowledge is your neighbor, in the Bible sense; and woe to you if you find sin there and suffer it!

See what God says to you through Ezekiel. "Son of man, I have made thee a watchman unto the house of Israel; therefore hear the word at My mouth, and give them warning from Me. When I say unto the wicked, Thou shalt surely die; and thou givest him not warning, nor speakest to warn the wicked from his wicked way, to save his life; the same wicked man shall die in his iniquity; but his blood will I require at thine hand." There is no "red tape" in those instructions; God recognizes only two people as He speaks—you and your neighbor—and He gives command and warning accordingly.

Nor was our Lord less explicit, though less terrible, when He warned us: "Moreover, if thy brother shall trespass" (the words "against thee" are not in the Sinai manuscript), "go and tell him his fault." Tell him as you would like to be told yourself: alone, faithfully, and lovingly, with the consciousness of being God's messenger, and speaking in His Spirit.

If he hears, "thou hast gained thy brother"; if not, "thou hast delivered thine own soul."

"Lord have mercy upon us, and incline our hearts to keep this law!"

Spiritualism

Regard not them that have familiar spirits, neither seek after wizards, to be defiled by them; I am the Lord your God (Lev. 19:31).

A bright, keen-witted New England girl was a regular attendant at my Holiness Meetings. She did not doubt her own sanctification, nor did any one else, and her testimony was always clear and bracing like a waft of air from her own white mountains.

But one day in answer to the usual salutation, "How is it with your soul today?" she gave a defiant look, flushed scarlet, and waited for a full minute before a sharp "All right!" crisped on the air.

No, very wrong! What ailed her? By and by it came with a burst: "I've been to the spiritualist meeting down the street. Do you think they're wrong?"

"Spiritualists! Altogether so! And I get my ideas from the Bible. The Bible forbids our having anything to do with their meetings, their pretended miracles, or their teachings. Their own published works deny God and His word as we know them, entirely. But, tell me what effect they have had on you. Do you read your Bible any more since you have been to their meetings?"

"No," she admitted, "I don't read it at all. And I hardly pray once a week!"

"Do you love God, then, or work for souls any more?"

"No," impatiently. "I don't think about those things. I do want to know if they *can* materialize spirits so! I'm wild with curiosity."

We talked with each other more about it, and we talked with God, and the conclusions we reached were mainly these:

That good spirits were solely under the control of God, and that He sent them to this world on His own errands, as His Book showed, and at His own will—not at the call of "mediums," who repeated their messages and exhibited their faces for money!

That if the spirits were evil, we wanted no communication of any kind with them.

That if going to spiritualist meetings was counted by God worthy of physical death in Saul's day, its penalty would surely be spiritual death now. My girl was on the highway to prove this herself, since she had left off the very Bread of Life through her going.

And, lastly, that the logic, the reason, and the last word to be said on the subject, was to be found in God's message about it through Isaiah: "And when they shall say unto you, seek unto them that have familiar spirits, and unto wizards that peep, and that mutter: should not a people seek unto their God? On behalf of the living should they seek unto the dead [Revised Version]? To the law and to the testimony: if they speak not according to this word, it is because there is no light in them."

My girl saw the light, and turned to it again, picked up her neglected Bible, and promised to go no more to the halls of darkness.

A Help Becomes a Hindrance

And Moses made a serpent of brass, and put it upon a pole; and it came to pass, that if a serpent had bitten any man, when he beheld the serpent of brass, he lived (Num. 21:9).

Here was the thing ordained of God to stand as a type and symbol of His sacrificed Son. It was meant to help the people to a better understanding and love of God, and, at the time of ordering, did really prove of utmost blessing to them. And yet, six hundred years afterwards, they had turned it into an idol, and were rendering it the worship and fealty which belonged to God only!

So it may come to be with our cherished symbols and forms, which in the past have widened our narrow conception of God, strengthened our feeble faith, and helped to bring us health of soul. We Salvationists find the greatest help to spiritual growth in the uniform, the open speech and praying, the ardent and striking form of public worship which make so broad a mark of separation between us and the world. But the moment we cease to wear the uniform for God, and put it on only as the dress of The Salvation Army; when we follow our peculiar ceremonial only from custom; their value and usefulness have ended, they are likely to become a foolish and helpless idol.

The man who relies on a past experience for present Salvation worships "a thing of brass" no less than he who depends for his soul's safety on rites of baptism or confirmation. The man who argues out for himself Salvation from Hell by creed, instead of experiencing a daily Salvation from sin through the applied Blood of Jesus, worships an intellectual error instead of his Maker.

"Examine yourselves, whether ye be *in the faith*; prove your own selves."

A Prophet

The woman saith unto Him, Sir, I perceive that Thou art a prophet (John 4:19).

No need for a prophet to declare the fact. Let him speak the message of God burning in his soul, and the world will find him out, though it may deny his inspiration, and kill him.

A prophet is a man with a God-given word to the world—not necessarily a foreteller of things to come. He brings a message, and his business is to deliver it truly. He does not seek favor from man, but rather to please the One who sent him.

He speaks out of his heart. To him the things he speaks often seem commonplace enough; but to the uninspired they come with awful force, they astonish, arouse, and, according to the state of their heart, either enrage or enrapture those who hear.

Would you be a prophet? Can you drink of the cup that Jesus drank of, and be baptized with His baptism? Will you purge yourself, or, rather, will you consent for the Holy Ghost to purge you, of self-seeking, of a man-pleasing or a man-fearing spirit? Are you ready to be misunderstood, to be wounded in the house of your friends; to spend and be spent, though the more abundantly you love the less you be loved? Are you ready to be crucified? Can you count it all joy to suffer with Jesus?

Will you stop trying to say smooth things, smart things, great things, and consent to be a fool for Christ's sake, speaking the simple message that He gives? If so, He will make you one of His prophets.

The Basis of Faith

Except ye see signs and wonders, ye will not believe
(John 4:48).

The only way to see signs and wonders, is to believe. Faith must come first; then God works signs and wonders before the people, and puts critics and sceptics and philosophers to shame.

However, the soul must have some ground of faith, some evidence, before it believes, else faith would be a blind, unguided thing, without law or order.

The true ground of faith is the unchangeable character of God, and the simple conditions of submission and obedience to His will laid down in the Bible. God is love. He is just and true and holy. He desires the highest good of all men; He has declared this in His word, and has proved it in ten thousand ways, but most wonderfully in the sacrifice of His Son for us. He has also said, "If we ask anything according to His will He heareth us; and if we know that He hears us, whatsoever we ask, we know that we have the petitions that we desired of Him."

Here, then is the true basis of faith, and not any signs and wonders which may be given as a reward of faith. My business, when I desire a thing of God, is, first to find out if it is a thing consistent with His character and revealed will; then, I should search my heart to see if there is any hindrance in myself; and, being fully assured that it is the will of God, I should offer my petition in the sure expectation that it shall be granted. And, though the answer may be delayed, it is never denied.

While the basis of faith is God's revealed character and will—in other words, His word; yet the signs and wonders that follow and reward faith tend to strengthen and confirm it, and lead it to yet more noble and daring exercises.

This nobleman, not rebuffed by the declaration of Jesus, that he would not believe unless "he saw signs and wonders," still insisted that Jesus should come and heal his son. Jesus said to him, "Go thy way; thy son liveth. And the man believed the word that Jesus had spoken unto him, and he went his way." That is true faith—to believe the word of God, and act as if one believed it.

Look Well to Your Commission

He hath anointed Me . . . to preach the acceptable year of the Lord (Luke 4:18, 19).

There needs another fragment of text to make it clear what God took flesh upon Him to preach, and that fragment is, "Now is the accepted time."

Most Army Officers are beset, sooner or later, by zealous advocates of sectarian doctrines or reforms. They would have them give up preaching Salvation to talk about taxes—total abstinence—the keeping of some particular day as Sabbath— the coming of our Lord at a near date— or even some anti-Scriptural idea.

But look well to your commission, comrade. The Captain of our Salvation came "to preach the Gospel to the poor; . . . to heal the brokenhearted to preach deliverance to the captives, and recovering of sight to the blind, to set at liberty them that are bruised"—these are all included in that present Salvation of "the acceptable year of the Lord," and we are not sent after Him to lift any other standard. And if we preach faithfully the great Salvation from all sin, compelling all our world to hear it, there will be no time for any outside issues, even if we had liberty to proclaim them.

> The love of Christ doth me constrain
> To seek the wandering souls of men;
> With cries, entreaties, tears, to save,
> To snatch them from the gaping grave.

Cavilling Unbelief
and Honest Doubt

Whatsoever we have heard done in Capernaum, do also here in thy country (Luke 4:23).

The Lord works no miracles to gratify idle curiosity, nor to satisfy cavilling unbelief. He will not attempt to prove His divinity to those who are not willing to acknowledge it. He will leave them to find it out to their infinite confusion and everlasting shame in the great day of His appearing, when, whether they choose to do so or not,"every knee shall bow, and every tongue shall confess that Jesus Christ is Lord." "To the froward He will show Himself froward."

But where He finds an honest soul who wants to know the truth, yet is filled with doubts which it hates, He is willing to come in the meekness and lowliness of His heart with sufficient evidence to convince and banish doubts.

To King Herod, whose idle curiosity made him "exceeding glad" to see Jesus, "because he hoped to have seen some miracle done by Him," Jesus would answer not a word. To the chief priest and the mocking crowd who jeeringly said, "Let Christ the King of Israel descend now from the cross, that we may see and believe," He made no sign, and answered no word. But to honest, but doubting, Thomas, He said, "Reach hither thy finger, and behold My hands; and reach hither thy hand, and thrust it into My side, and be not faithless, but believing"; while at the grave of Lazarus He prayed, saying, "Father, I thank Thee that Thou has heard Me; and I knew that Thou hearest Me always; but because of the people which stand by I said it, that they may believe that Thou has sent Me."

Relaxing the Commandments

> *Whosoever therefore shall break one of these least commandments, and shall teach men so, he shall be called the least in the Kingdom of Heaven* (Matt. 5:19).

It used to puzzle me greatly, before God saved me, to read this verse, and to think that a man could break even the least of God's commandments, and teach others to break it, and have *any* place in His Kingdom. It seems more incredible now.

But Rotherham's translation shows the meaning of our Lord clearly: "Whosoever, therefore, may relax one of these commandments the least, and teach men in this way, shall be called least in the kingdom of the heavens."

It is not possible for a man to deliberately teach others to disregard the law of God, and enter that Kingdom; but there are many, in these days, who profess to be earnest followers of Jesus, who do both teach and follow a dangerous relaxing of the pure law of God.

Our Lord is addressing the Pharisees, who taught that the law might be divided into graver and lighter matters, just as some Churches not speak of "deadly" and "venial" sins. He has just spoken of the permanency of the law in every essential, and He shows that in no detail can its precepts be disregarded without danger to the soul

"But," you say, "human nature cannot bear it. No man can live up to this tremendous law. It reaches up to Heaven; it embraces the very grave; it covers the whole range of human thought, imagination, and experience; and demands of us a moral perfection which it is not in nature to meet."

True. Then, let nature die, and let Almighty Grace take its place. That is God's wonderful plan for you; that is how

66

He restores to you again—by Jesus' life in you— all that you have lost through sin. *You* cannot keep this law without relaxing it greatly, but the One who made it can take possession of your will, and keep it through you. Put your will into His hands, and He will divinely empower it to keep His law, and will make you "do and teach" all His glorious commandments. The power is God's, but the choice and faith must be yours.

Do not try to bring the law down to meet your ability, comrade. That is "relaxing" it; but where the power you possess does not meet the understood requirements of God's word, go to Him and get the power.

The law says, "Cease from anger." Then, do not take refuge behind that much-abused term, "righteous indignation"; but say frankly to your Savior, "Lord, I have no power to keep this law. Remove the temper that hinders Thy writing it on my heart, and keep me from sinning against Thee."

The law says, "Thou shalt not bear any grudge against the children of thy people"; and, "Grudge not one against another, brethren, lest ye be condemned." I have seen people actually trying to cover their breach of this law with that great text in Ephesians, "Forgiving one another, even as God, for Christ's sake, forgave you." "But God forgave me," they say, "when I repented and confessed; I'll forgive her when *she* repents and confesses!"

They forget that God has always that forgiving spirit which He enjoins upon us, and that the forgiveness which can be ours only on conditions of confession and repentance is a judicial forgiveness, belonging to God only, and which can never be exercised by man. God's forgiveness cleanses the wrongdoer; your forgiveness can never make him pure, but will help to keep you so. But you must forgive like God, out of the abundance of your God-like love, hiding you enemy's sins away in its profound depths until they have sunk below your memory, and you can never any more "remember them against him, much less bring them up against him."

And so with the whole law. You cannot keep it, but God can. My baby cannot form a single letter, but I can put the pencil in her fingers, guide her little, helpless hand to write clearly and well whatever I wish. God can do the same with your will. Put it into His sole possession, and He can trace with it a perfect copy of His pure law in your life, and make of you a living epistle that men shall read with conviction and profit, and He and His angels with great joy.

Fishers of Men

And Jesus said unto them, Come ye after Me, and I will make you to become fishers of men. And straightway they forsook their nets, and followed Him. . . . And straightway He called them: and they left their father Zebedee in the ship with the hired servants, and went after Him (Mark 1:17-20).

A soldier had felt for some time that he must some day go into the Work, and promised God that he would go whenever he was called. He was master of his time, and had no arrangements to make. The call came while his hammer was lifted to strike a blow, and he obeyed it instantly. "The blow never fell, and before noon he had sold his kit of tools and was ready. For years he has been a successful Officer, and is daily increasing in the gifts and graces of those whom God calls to be leaders.

Does God call you? Them let nothing hinder you, but go, and God will be with you, as He was with Moses and Paul. As years speed by you will be increasingly thankful to Him that no business prospects, no fond friendships, no longing for power, no love of secluded ease kept you from the battle's front with its burdens and bitter conflicts, its sorrows, and its soul-satisfying triumphs.

One soul saved from Hell through your labors will pay for all your toil; one look at the face of Jesus will reward you for all your privations. What care Peter and John now if they did lose all they had dear when they began to follow Jesus; if they did suffer to death for the men they sought to save? And what will you care?

To the natural heart, and unsanctified mind, the commands of God are foolishness. "Get thee out from thy kindred, and from thy father's house, unto a land that I will show thee," said God to Abraham. How foolish to leave home and wealth and greatness to go to a land that he knew not! But Abraham believed, obeyed, and became heir of greater possessions.

"I will send thee unto Pharaoh, that thou mayest bring forth My people the children of Israel out of Egypt," was God's word to Moses. What folly for this poor shepherd, who, forty years before, had fled from Pharaoh's face a condemned murderer, to try and deliver a nation of slaves from the iron hand of the mightiest monarch of earth! But he believed and obeyed, and God humbled the proud king to the dust, and the nation of slaves was freed.

God sent Paul to the Gentiles to "open their eyes, and to turn them from darkness to light, and from the power of Satan unto God." Think of it! One man, belonging to a conquered, despised, hated people, sent to the proud, idolatrous nations, with the message that a crucified Jew was the Son of God, the Savior of the world, and that there was no Salvation except in His name. What foolhardiness for this man, without wealth, national prestige, political power, or social favor, to start out in the face of religious hatred and national and political antagonism, to convert a lost world to this new faith of the day! But he "was not dis-

obedient to the heavenly vision." He went, and the Holy
Ghost went with him. He went to unparalleled toils and
sufferings, but he won unparalleled victories and heavenly
joys and consolations; and God helped him to do much to
win the world to Himself.

Does your call to work for God seem foolish, unreasonable, impossible? "Have faith in God." Obey, and, like
Abraham, Moses, and Paul, you will yet praise Him for
each step of the way He led you, and for the part He gave
you to do in the world's redemption.

Concerning Honor

*How can ye believe, which receive honor one of
another, and seek not the honor that cometh from
God only* (John 5:44)?

Jesus simply means this: "How can you receive the gift
of God when you are so perfectly satisfied with, and so
busy receiving what man can give you?

The promise is to those who "hunger and thirst"; but
how can he who is content with what he has, thirst for
what he has not? Not till a man sees Jesus to be infinitely
desirable will He receive Him; and Jesus never seems
infinitely desirable till we see ourselves lost for ever without Him. Then honor from men is no more to us than the
sparkling bubble on the crest of the engulfing wave to the
wrecked and struggling mariner.

But shall a man receive no honor from his fellow men?
No! not unless he is sure God sent it to him through them;
and in that case he will return the honor to God, and take

none of the glory to himself, and he will be as content to lose it as to receive it. Daniel received honor from man; but he willingly laid it aside, together with life itself, when the glory of God demanded it, and his loyalty to God was laid in the balance against it.

These words were spoken especially to the leaders, and those in authority. How hard it is for those who lead the people to receive their honor came to them, or if they have lost Him after their promotion! I knew an Officer high up in The Army ranks who could not get sanctified till he was willing to confess to every Officer and Soldier under him that he had never previously been sanctified.

The confession had to be made, and instead of being met with contempt which Satan suggested, it was received with joy; the power of God fell on him and all who heard him, and great tides of victory swept throughout his command.

An earnest, fearless, loving minister of the Gospel, or Salvation Army Officer, will be loved and honored by the people who are blessed by his life and words. Paul was so honored and loved that he says of the Galatians, "Ye received me as an angel of God, even as Christ Jesus" But Paul did not seek this honor. He sought the honor that cometh from God only, and God added this honor from man.

Paul never sacrificed a principle to gain the goodwill of anyone. He did not hesitate to reprove or rebuke sin whatever the cost might be to him; and in Asia, where he had had his greatest successes (Acts 19), he lost the favor of the people rather than be unfaithful to their souls and to the trust God had committed to him. So in his old age he writes to Timothy, "All they which be in Asia are turned away from me." But the honor that cometh from God still remained to him.

Walk in the Spirit

For My yoke is easy, and My burden is light."(Matt. 11:30).

"Captain, I tell you, it is hard to be a Christian! That is what a young man once said to me and his gloomy brow and dejected attitude suggested that he had suffered much in making the discovery.

"I do not find it so," I said. "It seems to me the easiest thing in the world. And I have the same Devil to fight that you have; the same world against me; and my flesh isn't any different, except that a woman's nerves are usually worse than a man's."

"Oh, you!" he answered, expressively, "You are an Officer. That's very different."

"The difference is not in my favor, then. You have to work with your hands, and I with my head; but your way pleases you best. And you have as sweet and amiable a wife as a man could wish, a beautiful baby, and a comfortable home. It is not your circumstances that make your trouble, my brother."

"No, it is my temptations," he admitted. "I always have to be watching my temper, and I am not contented, though I have nothing to complain of. I feel like an angel in the Meetings, but I do get the 'blues' outside. I thought it was going to be always easy and pleasant, and it is not. It is hard, I say, to be a Christian!"

Paul explains this poor fellow's difficulty in simple words: "For the flesh lusteth against the Spirit, and the Spirit against the flesh; and these are contrary the one to the other; so that ye cannot do the things that ye would." War to the death is neither "easy" nor "pleasant"! How can it be? But how to end it? Paul tells the way out of this state of affairs as simply as he states the case, and in the same

72

chapter of Galatians. "Walk in the Spirit," he says, " and ye shall not fulfil the lusts of the flesh."

My Soldier had been soundly converted, and God was greatly using him, but the "body of sin" was beginning to make itself more and more felt in him. As is but natural, the presence of two opposing forces in his spiritual nature made havoc with his peace. Is it so with you?

"Walk in the Spirit," advised Paul. That Spirit will always bring you, in any doubt or difficulty, to your knees before God: it will lead you to search His word for the cause of trouble, and it will make clear His will to you.

This Soldier had only to put his confession of discontent and despondency against the commands of God, "Be content with such things as ye have," and "Rejoice evermore," to be convicted by the Spirit of his heart uncleanness; that is, of his unlikeness to God. Then, walking in that Spirit, he would have come to the strait gate of self-crucifixion, leading to resurrection like in Jesus.

Once dead to self, he would be living his life in harmony with God's will, doing God's work in God's way instead of his own. All his unrest would have given way to a settled peace; the discord in his soul would have resolved itself into harmony; his darkened sky would have been filled with fairest sunshine, and he would have proved the words of Jesus, "My yoke is easy," entirely true, and so would have found it easy to be a Christian.

Being a Christian is not an episode in a life. It is the life itself. All other things, including our daily work, are but its incidents; they are a small and comparatively trifling part of our real life. But, if bread-winning or time-killing or anything else, constitutes our life, and following God is in our hearts, only secondary, it is indeed a hard thing to do, because it is reversing God's natural and easy order. Put things in their proper order: "Seek first the kingdom of God and His righteousness" and then, "with joy shall ye draw water from the wells of Salvation.

Idle Words

But I say unto you, That every idle word that men shall speak, they shall give account thereof in the day of judgment (Matt. 12:36).

What is an idle word? Rotherham translates the term "useless expression," and thereby cuts off some faint hopes of a wide tongue range from those of us who like to talk.

Solomon and James have pointed out the terrible dangers of foolish talking, in the most direct and simple language. And few of us have been Christians for long without suffering deep regret, and heartily repenting because of foolish things which we have said.

But how to get help? Say that we do use idle words, admit that we have said many things that the seen presence of Jesus would have silenced, how could we make sure of not doing it again and again?

First, let conviction do its thorough work by acknowledging your wrong-speaking as a sin—one against your soul, at least. You said nothing absolutely wicked; but did you not feel that the solemn, joyous Spirit within you was grieved by your trifling? Did your light talk leave you out of tune for praying with the comrades with whom you had been joking, or leave you "not in the mood" for immediate communion with God on your own account, or without a desire for your Bible "just at present"? Then, those same words grieved the Spirit, which alone makes the word of God of any value. "The words that I speak unto you, they are Spirit"; and if your own words have created in you even a passing and slight distaste for the Bible, it is because in just that measure, however minute, your spirit is at variance with His. Give your trouble its right name; then you will not be trying after reform, but seeking for cure.

Malachi explains the method of cure: "My covenant was with him of life and peace; I gave them to him for the fear wherewith he feared Me, and was afraid before My name. The law of truth was in his mouth, and iniquity was not found in his lips."

God's covenant with man includes, you see, the power to talk in a way that pleases God. That is implied, too, in the commands about Christian speaking. "Let your speech be always with grace, seasoned with salt." Always such as shall preserve you and others from sin, not lead you into it—always with something from God in it, though you talk about the cooking or typewriting. "Let your conversation be as it becometh the Gospel of Christ."

If you have never made with God the perfect covenant whose result in your life His Book calls "holiness," "sanctification," "a clean heart," "crucifixion with Christ," make it now, and let it include fire-cleansed lips such as Isaiah got thereby. And if the covenant has been made, and the lips not included in your part of it, offer them up at once.

David did. "I am purposed," he said, "that my mouth shall not transgress"; and then he prayed with faith: "Set a watch, O Lord, before my mouth; keep the door of my lips." And God has put it on record that David pleased Him.

So may you please God. The promises and commands as well as the examples prove it, and the glorious result is written down by Malachi, "He walked with Me in peace and equity, and did turn many away from iniquity."

Take Heed What You Hear

And He said unto them, Take heed what ye hear: with what measure ye mete, it shall be measured to you: and unto you that hear shall more be given (Mark 4:24).

The Lord Jesus had just been telling His disciples that "the seed was the word"; and now in the same connection, He warns them to take heed what they hear. May there be danger, then, in listening to Bible reading and Bible talk?

Yes, undoubtedly, when those things, which ought always to be for our building up in the faith and knowledge of God, are used to draw our attention away from Him and His Salvation to merely sectarian doctrines, and "questions and strifes of words," "foolish and unlearned questions," which "do gender strifes." The word of God was given us for life and growth, to make us like Jesus, and any use of it which does not tend directly to these ends is forbidden by this most forcible warning.

I have met many a sanctified Congregationalist, Baptist, Episcopalian, Methodist; but labels were needed to tell to which sect each belonged; they had all but one theme, and that was the great Salvation of God.

But when the idle words of sectarianism are blowing, we need not listen to the sound they make. If you do not hear the pure Gospel, leave those who speak. You have no right to endanger your soul's health and peace. "Take heed what ye hear," because to you who listen to "the truth," even the very message of Jesus' Salvation, "shall more be given."

But this command is of broader application than to our mere hearing of the word of God. We are not always hearing the Bible expounded, or even referred to; but alas! much of the time we must be hearing something, and to the everyday talk of friends and acquaintances we must, for our soul's safety and well-being, apply this counsel from God.

Do not listen to gossip, scandal, backbiting, detraction, foolish jesting, malicious hints. "Avoid profane [worldly] and vain babbling," wrote Paul to a young Christian, because, he tells him, "they will increase unto more ungodliness, and their word will eat as doth a canker.

But, suppose you must hear these things? One is often shut up in a street car or railway carriage with chatterers whose loud voices compel one to listen; or, still worse, one has sometimes to live with people such as Paul warns us against associating with.

Then, "take heed how ye hear." If the outward ear must listen, keep the heart turned to God, keep your mind stayed upon Him, and never for an instant let your will assent. It is not a mental attitude of resistance to what you hear that will help you—safety can only be found in the turning of the soul to God, and reposing upon Him and His promises for all your need.

Make a covenant with your ears, as David did with his eyes, and the ever-hearing God will keep you from falling through any snare of words.

Faith, Not Feelings

O thou of little faith, wherefore didst thou doubt (Matt. 14:31).

It is not written that Peter ever testified in a Meeting: "For three years I lived an up-and-down Christian life, before I got where the Devil couldn't shake me"; but he might have done so, and have instanced this experience on the lake as an example of what he meant. How faith and doubt chased each other through Peter's heart in the very sight and sound of his Savior!

"It is I," said Jesus; "be not afraid."

"Lord, if it be Thou," cried back the unbelieving disciple. Faith knows no "ifs"; still, at the word of command Peter walked out, in an uplift of feeling mingled with a little faith.

So long as he kept his eyes on Jesus, all went well; but, after a few unaccustomed steps, the flash of feeling died down, and he began to consider his unfavorable circumstances. He had thought only of Jesus when he set out, and in that fact lay his miraculous power to obey the seemingly impossible command of God.

Is not the experience of Peter something like yours? At your conversion you set out with a glad love for your Lord which shut out every worldly consideration from your mind; you did what He told You to do without a thought of anything but His compelling love; you followed His will as naturally and as exactly as steel filings follow a magnet. Then, when the first flush of emotion passed, you began to listen to the idle talk of people—to the wind's blowing! Just as Jesus made the waves over which faith in Him was carrying Peter—or "without Him was nothing made that was made"—so He made and ordered the circumstances in which you were living. The word of command which He spoke to you would have empowered you to go on in spite of all, just as that word would have brought Peter safely over, though the waves had tossed mountains high.

But you looked away from Him, and a black sky of opposition, a curling wave or two of difficulty, terrified you; your impulse pined, like a butterfly out of the sunshine; your unused faith loosed its weak hold when you looked and listened to others beside Jesus, and down you went—a sad spectacle to angels, and a sorry example to other baby souls about you.

O thou of little faith, wilt thou rid thyself of that mysterious something which every now and again makes against God? If you have in the past been like Peter on the lake, become now like Peter after Pentecost—able through the Spirit to keep your rightful vows, and to carry out God's will for you.

Death to Self-Will

For I came down from Heaven, not to do Mine own will, but the will of Him that sent Me (John 6:38).

The one great object lesson of all time is set forth in this verse that God's children may study it, and live thereby. God's humanity was assumed that it might be utterly subjected to His Spirit, and that we might learn by that wonderful example how to become God-like ourselves.

"Not to do Mine own will." The setting aside of our own will is the first step for us in following Jesus. Self-will began to develop in our cradles, it grew past our growth, and, long before we had attained full stature, to gratify it seemed the end and object of our lives. Its power was crippled and diminished when we were converted, but still we had to recognize a mighty force remaining within us whose occasional assertions of mastery quelled everything else, and grieved the Spirit of God away from our troubled hearts.

And now what is demanded of us? To put down this once dominant will for ever. We seemed born into the world to secure our own way; but Jesus came down from Heaven "not to do" His own will. Ah, self, this bodes a bitter death for you!

> A tempest on my heart was falling,
> A living cross this was to be!
> I struggled sore, I struggled vainly,
> No other light mine eyes could see.

There is no other. If there had been an easier way by which to lead us to purity, to a peace and joy which cannot be shaken, the love of Jesus would have chosen it. But there was none, and His fathomless love took the way of the cross. Its beams and nails bring death to our human nature in the hour when we, too, lay down our will.

If your self-pitying heart still falters, look at the motives. On the one hand, to escape from sin, and its consequence, multiplying miseries; on the other hand, to be lastingly like Jesus, a continual sharer of His serene, unearthly joy.

Your will is your life, and "whosoever will save his life shall lose it; but whosoever will lose his life for My sake, the same shall save it." Here is policy; here is advantage; here is eternal gain. But you must lay down your will as did Jesus, "through the Eternal Spirit"; and that Spirit will help you do it when you loathe yourself and your arrogant will, and long with all the force of your immortal being to be holy like your God.

Then, you can go on unhindered to do the will of God. And "this is the will of God, even your sanctification." He has never meant anything else for you but that you should be cleansed from all sin, filled with the Spirit, and kept from falling, until you stand before His throne of glory "with exceeding joy." That you should do your part, and believe on Him for this result, is His will for you now. Only believe Him this moment for your sanctification, and then go on all your days witnessing in your own heart and life the unspeakable glory of God.

Unprofitable Work

Every plant, which My Heavenly Father hath not planted, shall be rooted up (Matt. 15:13).

A girl sat with a face of despair over a long seam which had to be picked out and resewed, and another was trying to help and cheer her at the same time. "It is not hard work," she said, "and it will soon be done. And it all comes in with the day's work; you're not doing anything else when you're doing that."

"No," answered the victim of a mistake. "I am not mourning because it is hard, but because of the the time wasted. I hate doing things over again! I might be helping some one else, if I had not my own work to do again,"

There is a melancholy side to undoing any work but most of all in spiritual fields. Think of men and women toiling through the few years of this life to build up a temple of doctrinal straws, a high tower of dogmatic stubble, which cannot withstand the winds of time let alone the fire of God's judgment!

But what works will stand? What earthly plants can we set out and cherish that shall strike roots into the very nature of things here, and send enduring blossoms and fruit up into the heavenly ether?

It is only "faith which worketh by love" that "availeth anything" to those who are "in Christ Jesus" (Gal. 5:6). So any teaching, or preaching, or doing, which is not based on that love to man which comes from God, is Christ-like neither in its origin nor in its practice. It will not bear the tests of "the faith of the Son of God" (Gal. 2:20); it is not planted by Him, and must be rooted up. However fair its leafage and vigorous its growth, it is only a harmful weed.

The plants of God are plants of grace; their fruits are those of the Spirit; their growth and tendency is always towards eternal life.

A man was once pressing some sectarian doctrine upon a Salvationist, and was met with this question, "Do you consider a knowledge of that subject necessary for my Salvation?

"Well, no, not exactly that," returned the argumentative brother; "but it is true; it is in the Bible, and you ought to know about it."

"Did you know of any one getting saved or sanctified through talking about it?

"Not that I remember."

"Then I shall let it alone till the world is saved. I want all my talk to help my soul, or some one else's."

That rule is a good one to apply to the plants offered you by one and another for setting out in your spiritual garden. Remember that your short, precious life must be spent in their cultivation, and that the blessing and bane of all who come in contact with you will depend upon the fruit they bear. Will they help our soul, or the souls of others, to advance in the grace and knowledge of God?—that is the first question.

"The seed is the word," but many doctrines are based by men upon the word of God, and a meaning wrested from various texts to support them, which do not produce growth in the soul which accepts them. That is conclusive evidence that they are not of God; that they are parasites, and not the product of the fruit-bearing Vine. The truths of the Gospel increase godliness in the human soul as we ponder and talk about them. It is these truths which Paul called "good and profitable," and charged Timothy to "preach and exhort." It is the time-wasting, heart-perverting teachings of men which shall eventually "be rooted up."

God's Rate of Interest

And they did all eat, and were filled; and they took up of the broken meat that was left seven baskets full (Matt.15:37).

The rate of interest which God pays on our small invest-ments with Him is something astounding. The disciples gave over to Jesus their small stock of seven little loaves, expecting to see them disappear among the hungry thou-sands in a moment, and certainly not looking for any return. But they probably had a far larger dinner than the seven loaves would have furnished, when they shared their miraculous increase with the crowd, and had remaining seven baskets full for dinners to come!

God pays at that rate still. He does not confine Himself to the promised hundred-fold, but is better than His word to every child of His who trusts Him wholly. There are scores in every land when He is known who can testify that He multiplies all they have ever given Him, enriches others with it, and then returns it into their own posses-sion till their hands overflow. They have given wrecked lives, and received back happy ones; they have given unpeaceful homes, and received again joyful Heaven-like ones; they have given unused powers, and received pleasure even greater than the profit from the use God has made of them; they have given money, food, and clothing, and have received their kind back again in greater value—peace and joy from Heaven which are beyond all reckoning.

Yet they all gave—as the disciples did their bread—expect-ing nothing again, ungrudgingly, joyfully, because Jesus asked it of them.

God's Purpose in Clouds

While He thus spake, there came a cloud, and overshadowed them; and they feared as they entered into the cloud (Luke 19:34).

Does it not seem strange that these two disciples could have been afraid to enter a cloud, however dark and foreboding it might appear, when Jesus was there with them, under their very eyes, within hearing of their voices and reach of their hands?

But the disciples had to learn, as, maybe, some of us have also, that even sight and hearing are useless to keep the heart without faith.

They had plenty of feeling—they loved their Lord, and their quick emotions made them swear to die with Him when danger was threatening. But their faith was feeble and imperfect, and consequently their love lacked the vigor that "casteth out fear." They were afraid to face death when it came near, as shown when their boat was likely to be wrecked; and they were afraid of an overhanging cloud, although they heard the very voice of God coming from its dark depths.

God's purpose in sending the cloud was to make a new revelation of Jesus to the disciples, and to let them hear His comforting, cheering helping voice as they could not have heard it otherwise. But His loving words fell upon fearful, doubting hearts; and even the words of Jesus cannot profit unless "mixed with faith in them that heard."

God has no other purpose in sending clouds over you, my comrade. And if you cannot help fears and doubts overwhelming you when the sunshine is obscured, it is because you have not yet let Him sanctify you wholly. "He that feareth is not made perfect in love."

"Servant of All"

If any man desire to be first, the same shall be last of all, and servant of all (Mark 9:35).

The race has grown less childish in the centuries since Jesus thus spoke to the men who were exchanging hot words about their own greatness. We no longer dispute rudely over precedence and position. But the devilish fruits of rivalry and self-exaltation are as abundant in the hearts of men today—are as contrary to the Spirit of God as they were then, and need to meet their death by the sword of this word of Jesus.

"Last of all." Who will see you, down at the foot of life's procession, and deal out that praise of man on which self in you has been battening? No one at all; and very likely you will only get contempt and hard words from the very people for whose sake you have sacrificed yourself. But this is exactly the treatment that Jesus received when He became nothing in the eyes of men for your sake. When you take the lowest place possible to you for His sake, you have fellowship with Jesus in His humility, in His joy of self-sacrifice, and of pleasing God.

"And servant of all." Jesus came into the world for the purpose of being a servant (Mark 10:45). Is it the object of your inmost heart to be like Him in this; or is there a desire for rank, for privilege, for power other than that of the pure Spirit of God?

It seems a trifle to want a front seat on the platform, to desire a little promotion, to care for a bit of privilege above that of the very lowest and least in the ranks. So the minute red spot which a rattlesnake's bite leaves on your skin looks a mere trifle; but it indicates death working secretly in the veins, and unless you check the poison with and antidote, that tiny spot will work your death.

To be *really* first of all is to be like Jesus, and that likeness consists in lowliness, humility, self-obliteration. A man cannot take up the practice of these graces as he would the daily practice of gymnastics; they must be the involuntary outcome of the Spirit that is in him. There is a "voluntary humility" which Paul warns us against—forcing ourselves to do hard, unpleasant, or humbling things in order to produce the graces of Jesus in us. But such things can only harm us, by begetting a false confidence in our own piety and a trust in our own works instead of in our Savior.

Doing and Knowing

If any man will do His will, he shall know of the doctrine, whether it be of God (John 7:17).

> The light of reason cannot give
>   Life to my soul;
> Jesus alone can make me truly live,
> One glance of His can make my spirit whole;
> On this poor longing, wishing heart of mine,
>   Arise and shine!

One meets everywhere people who are much troubled about this, that, or the other commonly received doctrine of the Bible. They do not know whether the Bible is all inspired—they cannot tell if Jesus is Divine—or they are not sure about the future state. And they carry about these crushing uncertainties, all unconscious, apparently, of the beautiful and easy test provided by God for resolving their doubts. They shall *know* if they will but *do* the will of God.

But suppose, for instance, one is not certain that Jesus was very God, how is he to "do the will of God" so as to become clear on that point?

First of all, stop all arguing, and mere mental inquiry into the subject, and seek God as He tells you to do in the fifth chapter of Amos. Seek Him as a soul repenting of its sins, and yearning above everything else to be made pure. You want the truth? Then seek God for His Spirit, because He has promised that the Spirit shall lead you into all truth, and that He shall testify of Jesus; prove Him as God.

When once your will is put into God's hands, together with all your cherished beliefs and unbeliefs, leaving you free and ready to receive into your heart whatever He reveals to you, and you go on from that starting point to be taught of God, you will learn for yourself that He is Love, that He is ineffably tender and gracious, long-suffering, and merciful! You will be overwhelmed by the sight of His purity, His wisdom, His condescension, and you will find that you can only apprehend His glorious heart of love as He made it apparent by taking on Him the body and name of Jesus.

Search for orders daily where God has revealed His will in the Bible; and walk in every ray of light as fast as it reaches you. Ask Him for truth, for the knowledge of Himself, and expect to receive them. And when the old, haunting doubts return, hand them over at once to God, asking Him to keep you from them, and to continue in you the trustful heart of a little child.

"The Harvest is Great—Pray Ye"

The harvest truly is great, but the laborers are few:
pray ye therefore the Lord of the harvest, that He

would send forth laborers into His harvest (Luke
10:2).

Comrade, are you praying this prayer, as Jesus has commanded?

Perhaps you pray that other prayer of His teaching—"Our
Father"— in the solemn stillness of your own closet. But
remember that Jesus gave us that prayer because it was
asked for; He commanded us to pray for soul-winners out
to His own infinite understanding of the world's needs.
And when He had commanded His disciples to pray for
laborers, He *sent them.*

> Oh haste to help ere we are lost!
>   Send forth evangelists in spirit strong,
> Armed with Thy word, and dauntless host,
>   Bold to attack the rule of ancient wrong;
> And let them all the earth for Thee reclaim,
> To be Thy Kingdom, and to know Thy name.

Our Father

*No man knoweth . . . who the father is, but the Son,
and he to whom the Son will reveal Him* (Luke 10:22).

All nations of this world, both civilized and barbarous,
have a God of some kind, but their God is mostly a cold,
hard, unloving Force—a Cause—a Source of Law. The God
of merely nominal Christians is no better than a stern mag-
istrate, the author of a set of rules which they hate to keep,
and could not keep if they wished, while they remain as
they are. So that our Lord states only a general truth, attest-

ed both by the history and experience of mankind, when He says here that no man can apprehend the nature of God by his intellect alone.

We are told as children that God made the worlds, and as adults we accept the statement because no other adequate cause for the daily marvels of the near earth and the distant universe can be found or suggested. But to accept God as a Creator does not reveal Him to us as a Father. We can never know Him as Love, never understand His real nature and His feelings towards us, till we see Him taking our flesh upon Him; bearing our burdens, our sorrows, and our sins, living with us, dying for us, in the body called Christ Jesus. Only the Son can reveal Him. Do you remember how, when you were a little one, your own father represented not only all power but all tenderness to you? If you were frightened, you sheltered in his arms; if you were lonely, he comforted you; and when your child's heart felt a thrill of love and tenderness, it sought and found a full return from him.

God loves us more than that. Multiply the tenderest father's power of self-sacrificing love by infinity—and that is how God loves. But how to show it to our witless, stupid souls!—how was He to make us know that unmeasured love and pity and sympathy, and every gracious quality which our hungry hearts demand from some source perpetually, exist for us in Him?

Just as our fathers showed their love by stooping to our level, by becoming children with us, by incessant care and pains in all details of our need, so the Father of fathers has done for His children. He took our flesh, with its possibilities of pain, hunger, temptation, and weakness, upon Him; He put Himself into our possible circumstances—of poverty, homelessness, friendlessness; came to the level of the outcast by law as well as by misfortune, and ended His life of fellowship with sorrow and suffering by the most horrible of deaths. And this He did that in every place and cir-

cumstance where a soul might ever be found, it might realize, in just that condition of things, the infinite, compassionate love of God.

Love must always express itself by sacrifice. Whether it
be the love of parent, lover, or friend, sooner or later it
meets and stands the test of sacrifice; and we may search
not only the world of fact, but that of imagination, to parallel the sacrifice of God when He gave Himself to live
among us and die for us. And this sacrifice of Jesus, His
condescension, His endurance, His surrender, His loss,
measures, so far as can be done, His infinite love.

But there is no measure which can fix a limit to His
love; the mind staggers and fails as it attempts to fathom it.
He was "the God of consolation, but He came "acquainted
with sorrow"; He was "the glorious Lord," yet He hid not
His "face from shame and spitting"; He was "the mighty
One of Israel," yet He became "a worm and no man"; He
was "the Lord high over all," but became "a reproach of
men, and despised of the people," that we of little soul
might understand His love, His personal, burning, tender
love for us.

"Who Is My Neighbor?"

But he, willing to justify himself, said unto Jesus,
And who is my neighbor (Luke 10:29)?

This man, who came asking an insincere question,
received, although he did not care for it, a full and invalu-
able answer. He had been well taught as to the way to
Heaven, and might now have been traveling swiftly along

it, for he mapped out the route glibly and correctly from the Book itself: "Thou shalt love the Lord thy God with all thy heart, and with all thy soul, and with all thy strength, and with all thy mind; and thy neighbor as thyself."

"Thou hast answered right," said the Lord. " This do, and thou shalt live."

To be living now, that is the main point. The children of the world want a Salvation for the future; to be saved, not from sin, but from its inevitable and acknowledged consequences. But Jesus told the lawyer, and tells us through him, that eternal life begins here or nowhere. Eternity does but continue the processes wrought in time. There is no creation beyond the grave, no alteration—only continuance. "He that is righteous, let him be righteous still; and he that is filthy, let him be filthy still."

This man, who had the chance to ask things from Jesus, and to get answers, frittered it away in evasive talk; he "sought to justify himself," not to learn vital truths. "Who is my neighbor?" he asked.

So Jesus showed him that his neighbor was any human being whom he happened to come across that needed to be helped by him. The "neighbor" of the good Samaritan was a man he had never seen before, and might never see again; represented in your case, perhaps, by the insurance agent, patent medicine vender, or ragman, who drops in on you of a morning. But, having once met, even in such a casual way, the relation of "neighbor" is established, and the opportunity must be dealt with, either in the Samaritan or the Levite-and-priest fashion.

Again, the Samaritan had to go out of the ordinary course to be truly neighborly to the needy man. He took something on himself which did not properly belong to him; he meddled in the private affairs of a stranger! But he saved the man's life by it. And many a soul is saved by what the world calls spiritual meddling.

I have seen a wandering foot pedlar and a fruit-tree agent

go on their way in tears after some neighborly dealing about their souls by a passing stranger, and have seen many a rough man softened and touched by the interest shown in his Salvation by some one whom it was improbable he would meet again till the day of Judgment. But, Oh, the meeting of earthly neighbors there will be at the Bar!

Comrade, what sort of neighbor are you to the souls God gives you a chance to every now and again? The Man, who showed this lawyer his duty to the dying world about him, will question you some day about *your* neighbor. Shall you rank then with those who saw souls dying all along the way of life, but went by, looking after their own business? Or can you look Him in the face, and say, "Lord, the oil and wine of the Kingdom which You gave me, I used all the way for You?"

The News of the Day

There were present at that season some that told Him of the Galileans, whose blood Pilate had mingled with their sacrifices. And Jesus answering said unto them, Suppose ye that these Galileans were sinners above all the Galileans, because they suffered such things? I tell you, Nay; but, except ye repent, ye shall all likewise perish (Luke 13:1-3).

There is no indication in these verses that the people who brought this story to Jesus were in any way malicious or slandering in their talk; they were simply relating to Him a bit of harmless news. But our Lord seems to have taken no interest in accidents and horrors, *merely as such.* He was perfectly interested and compassionate about trifles when He could help or comfort or bless.

It seems clear that one of the many lessons we are to draw from the way in which our Lord received the news of the day, is this: that we are not to take in news from people or papers which cannot in any way profit either us or those with whom we have to do. When a great catastrophe sweeps hundreds of souls into eternity, and moves the civilized world with pity, one cannot help hearing about it, and reading the details may stir one up to more praying for the world, or furnish a moral for the Meeting. But the habitual filling of one's mind with the accidents and happenings of the day cannot profit.

Could you thank God for your newspaper, and ask Him to bless the reading of it to your soul?—and do you do these things? Did you care as much for the newspaper when God first saved your soul as you do now, or did your Bible absorb your spare time, and form your chief interest in reading? Does the old Book interest you less, now that you have become a daily reader of secular newspapers?

These are questions which you cannot afford to pass lightly by. Put them to your soul before God, and see if His Spirit will not prompt you hereafter to store your mind with the truths which will feed you to all eternity, instead of "lies, vanity, and things wherein there is no profit."

Count the Cost

So likewise, whosoever he be of you that forsaketh not all that he hath, he cannot be My disciple (Luke 14:33).

Did the Lord Jesus preach Holiness? A Christian of many years' standing asked me this question. "I know there is a great deal about it in the Bible, but did the Lord Himself preach it?

Without a doubt. John Wesley might well have founded his directions to his ministers to preach the doctrine of Sanctification by faith, "strongly, explicitly, and continually," upon the words of our Lord alone.

What, for example, could be either stronger or more unmistakable than His teaching in this chapter on the subject of Holiness? "If any man come to me"—"and whosoever cometh I will in no wise cast out"—there is still something beyond that; he must hate his own dearest, and his own life, in comparison with the love he bears God—must choose God and His will before all—or he cannot be the disciple (the learner) of Jesus.

Does that seem a hard doctrine to you? When Jesus preached the life of faith to His disciples in Galilee, some "went back and walked no more with Him." "It is a hard doctrine, who can hear it?" But others rose to the spiritual plane to which He was trying to lead them, and it may be your soul and many another has been blessed since then, because of their faith and self-abandonment.

All through His ministry the Lord Jesus preached Holi--ness with His human lips, but its teaching throughout the Bible is as much attributable to Him as the words which He spoke. His authority attaches to one part as well as to another. He is "the Word." He confirmed and established the whole moral and spiritual law of the Old Testament, and His Spirit dictated the whole inspired record.

It cannot be said too often, that Sanctification is something more than a distinguishing tenet of a religious sect. It is an experience; it is a life; and it is as such that Jesus and the prophets taught it. It is the high privilege of every child of God, bought for them by the shed Blood, included in the covenant with the fathers, and constituting the fitness of the soul for Heaven.

"My experience is a poor one: I'm not satisfied with it. I ought to be sanctified," said a sorrowful Christian yesterday.

Consider that! A child of God, going along in presence of the "cloud of witnesses," poor in faith, and consequently poor in good works—with faint and intermittent joy—with broken and uncertain peace—with spotted robe, starless crown, silent tongue, and clouded, downcast face! Such a sight must be cheering to devils, discouraging to men, pitiful to the angels, grieving to the Father

"Count the cost of not being sanctified," she was answered. "You will surely backslide if you are not; and who knows how many others will fail of the Kingdom through you? Is not that what Jesus meant in that talk in the fourteenth of Luke when He said we must forsake all to be His disciples, and warned us to count the cost?

"Yes, I believe it is. But the fear of man hinders me. I would have to testify in that dead church at home, and it's so hard!"

If she would only sit down and count the cost; would see whether she could afford, with only one soul to risk on the issue, to go against her conscience, against the command of God, against the warnings of Jesus—to please the few people in her church rather than to please her Savior and the hosts of Heaven, she would assuredly let God complete in her the work He had begun.

But will you?

The Time of Thy Visitation

*For the days shall come upon thee, that thine enemies
shall cast a trench about thee, and compass thee
round, and keep thee in on every side. And shall lay
thee even with the ground, and thy children within
thee; and they shall not leave in thee one stone upon
another; because thou knewest not the time of thy
visitation* (Luke 14:4, 44).

They might have known; and in that fact lay their sin.
They went on their own path, doing the works of God in
their own way, looking into the future for a Messiah to fit
their own ideas, while the words of the promised One
sounded in their streets. They searched the books of the
prophets for comfort while the Fulfillment of the Covenant
spoke in their synagogues unheeded. They demanded truth
while the words of Jesus fell on them like summer rains.

It was the day of their visitation, as today is of yours,
poor unsanctified soul. The long line of His promises reaches down to you from the Garden of Eden, the great roll of
His commandments is spread on every page of your Bible;
the testimony of those whom He has cleansed and kept
descends to you from every age. Yet you walk on coldly,
showing to the world of sinners about you what indiffer-
ence towards God's laws is possible in a child of His,
instead of displaying to them His power "to save to the
uttermost."

Your backsliding is foretold in these sad verses, and the
pitiful fall of some souls you love. And you do not believe
that the Heart which bled over Jerusalem weeks today over
the same blindness in you.

Glorify Thy Name

Now is my soul troubled; and what shall I say?
Father, save Me from this hour? But for this cause
came I unto this hour. Father, glorify Thy name (John
12:27, 28 [R.V]).

Rotherham puts in the text, and the Revised Version in the margin, the second interrogation mark, which some think, is needed to give the right meaning to this passage. They think that our Savior said, "Shall I ask My Father to save Me from this hour? Nay! for this purpose I came into the world. I ask nothing for My own poor body; but, Father, glorify Thy name!"

He had taken upon Him flesh like ours; and, even as ours would, it shrank from shame and torment, and a hideous parting with its spirit. He faced the unbelief, the scorn, the crucifying, not only of His own day, but of the ages to come; your sins and mine blackened the hour before Him. But He saw, beyond all these, that, if His flesh obeyed and endured to the end, God's love would be vindicated for the uttermost Salvation of the race, and so He cried out: "Father, glorify Thy name!"

Comrade, the hour from which Jesus was tempted to shrink foreshadowed such an hour for you. He put your temptation into words when He said, "Now is My soul troubled; and what shall I say? Father, save Me from this hour." And He shows you, in declaring the purpose of His earthly existence, that God has a loving, tender purpose in bringing you to the hour where you find only anguish and horror before you. God has brought you there in compassion and love and tender pity; meaning you to know, beyond all doubt, that His highest glory is merely and only your greatest good. Never forget that. God's glory is not a selfish, separate thing; it is nothing else than the utmost purification of your nature and its absorption into Himself. This you will realize throughout your whole being, when your will is wholly lost in the Divine will; when you can cry out, as Jesus did, in the very jaws of death, and the face of assaulting Hell, "Father, glorify Thy name!" Then you will hear the Voice that He heard, and you will realize as never before the unspeakable rapture of conscious union with the Triune God.

The Things That Are God's

Then saith he unto them, Render therefore unto
Caesar the things which are Caesar's, and unto God
the things which are God's (Matt. 22:21).

This word of Jesus, spoken to hypocrites, has yet a deep meaning for sincere and honest Christians. Such people pay Caesar easily enough. A soul with ever so light a measure of the Spirit of God will not carry a debt to man any longer than he absolutely must. But Oh, "the things which are God's that His children will keep for years hidden away where He has no use of joy of them, without any serious thought of "rendering" them! The time, the varied talents, the labor, given over to the world's use and profit, or rusting unused at all, which by Blood purchase, as well as by creative right, "are God's"!

How does one render his own to God? By the only worthy consecration—that which terminates in sanctification. The things which belong to God in you are your body, soul, and spirit; there is nothing of you which is not His, and which should not be duly rendered on His altar.

"Seek out the old way," when you mean to pay your debts to the Almighty; put your withheld will—your whole being—definitely on His altar, and believe that He accepts it. Then He will have His own shape to use, and He *will use it*, though it may not be at all in the way you had expected.

Think of the Christian world paying its debts to God—giving up all it is and all it has to His service! Once that were done, a steady stream of Officers and missionaries would go pouring into heathen lands, and the gladdest dreams of people who long to see Jesus reigning would be fulfilled.

You sing, "Grace there is my every debt to pay." Are you using the grace? Or, if you waited to make the song true, how long would there be a silence before your voice, your cornet or piano, would be heard again? Render to God, my comrade, what He has made you know belongs to Him, and you will find such peace and joy in your heart (no matter what storms rage outside) as in the past you never knew.

Unspoiled Uniform

But all their works they do for to be seen of men; they make broad their phylacteries, and enlarge the borders of their garments (Matt. 23:5).

It was a bad sign when the Jews took to altering their uniform. The simple distinctiveness of their ribbon border and fringe was lost when they exaggerated it into something elaborate and costly.

When the Salvationist, or any other uniform is constructed or altered "to be seen of men," instead of to please God, and signify a total abandonment to His service, its wearer has become a Pharisee at heart. "Do not ye after their works."

Watching

Watch therefore: for ye know not what hour your Lord doth come (Matt. 24:42).

When I was a tiny child, my mother found me perched in the south library window looking out intently at the distant road. "What are you doing there, child?" she asked.

"Watching for papa," I said; "it is almost time for him to come, and I want to see him the first one."

"But you are not ready," rejoined the sensible mother. "Look at your dirty hands, and that soiled apron. Papa wants to see his little girl clean, and he likes your hair shining. Go and get yourself ready for papa, and then take your papers and dolls' clothes off his table. I'm all ready for him, and so must you be."

It seems to me now that in spiritual matters her advice is still good for older children, and that her words show us exactly how we are to "watch" for our Lord. We are first to be ready ourselves, and then to make His earth ready as far as lies within our power. We have no business looking up to the clouds of heaven while our hearts will not bear the inspection of Him for whom we are looking. We have no leisure to study dates and times when the law of God for our daily lives is fulfilled in our hearts.

"Therefore, be ye also ready," said Jesus in this same talk. "Watching," in this sense, can have no practical meaning but getting ready, if we are not so; and keeping ready, if we are.

It is explained in other parts of the Holy Word how we are to be watching. "Watch unto prayer," admonishes Peter, "for the end of all things is at hand." Shall the end find us arguing with men about their opinions, instead of pleading with God for their Salvation?

"Watch thou in all things," Paul exhorted Timothy, just going into the work, and with great prospects of promotion before him. That is, the young officer was to watch Jesus continually, to test whether or not his life matched his Lord's. "Would the Lord speak so? Would Jesus do this, teach that, if He were in my place?" That is watching.

And the eyes that so look for Jesus in all matters of the daily life will see Him. Glory to God! They will not have to wait for His appearance in the clouds of glory, but they will behold Him in the clouds of heaviness which may shadow their everyday life; they will find His healing balm on every thorn which would pierce them; His tears mingling with every drop of sorrow their eyes pour down; His form bending under every cross appointed them, taking its weight and pain, and transforming it into a thing of joy. "Blessed are the pure in heart, for they," as they watch, "shall see God."

These Shall Go Away

And these shall go away into everlasting punishment; but the righteous into life eternal (Matt. 25:46).

The fear of death is an indestructible safeguard which God has set in our natures to protect the soul, and guide it into everlasting life. Men forget sometimes, they bluster often, but the Devil can neither destroy, nor long cover over, God's warning fear of death in their hearts. God loves them so; He longs so to save them that He has used every device possible to make them exercise their power of choice for their happiness and welfare. He has placed deep in the very springs of their being a desire for happiness in the future state, as well as a fear of coming punishment for sin. If men will but act under these motives according to God's revealed plan, they will not only secure perfect freedom from fears of every kind, but a degree of joy and satisfaction corresponding to all they ever imagined for the next world.

When God gave Himself in the body to die for us, the gift was once for all. Though He died a thousand times, the gracious deed would never move our hearts, if it does not now. He cannot become our Savior in any other world, if we will not accept Him as such in this. How should He? Will His love be any greater there than here? "I am the eternal God; I change not."

The whole universe cannot offer any better field than this earth where we shall have more or fairer chances to get deliverance from our sins. "Sin shall not have dominion over you." So that we are left without any excuse for committing sin.

But why, since we are mortal, must our punishment as sinners be eternal—why, when our bodies are dust, must their deeds go on inflicting lasting vengeance on the suffering soul?

Because it is the soul, consciously immortal, which commits sin against an Infinite God. It is not what we do in the body, but what we *are in heart* (only indicated outwardly through the body), that separates us of our own accord from God. David realized this, when, after ruining a woman and killing a man, he cried out, "Against Thee, Thee only, have I sinned, and done this evil in Thy sight."

His soul had wronged God's purity, his will had wronged the life, and he cried from out the abyss of his separation from God, rightly estimating Hell and Heaven. The gulf between right and wrong is bottomless; the anguish of wrong that might have been right can only end when wrong becomes right—and that will be never.

De Ravignan has put the truth with most startling clearness: "There is an absolute identity between Hell and sin; sin is voluntarily committed, Hell is voluntarily incurred; Hell and sin are equally the loss of God. The soul may be unconscious of this on earth; but becomes conscious of it in Hell, where the truth must be accepted. God does not choose eternal fire for the lost soul; it had voluntarily separated itself from Him, and He leaves it where it had placed itself, far from Him. God does not touch the soul; He leaves it, and its Hell begins."

Sanctified Lips

By this shall all men know that ye are My disciples, if ye have love one to another (John 13:35).

Love is manifested in many ways, but the most common ways are by speech and action. Men will judge, and rightly so, whether we love our comrades or not, by the way we talk about them. "Speak evil of no man" is what love has commanded us; but how often we hear an unkind word, a disparaging remark, a discreditable report, about one towards whom the speaker is specially bound to display love—a comrade.

A hungry and disappointed seeker after Holiness came to me the other night. "The trouble is, I have never seen it lived out," she said. "I know I have no right to look at people, but how can I help it when there's such an awful inconsistency between their testimony and their daily talk? The other night, in our Church Meeting, a woman who had given a beautiful, clear testimony to Holiness in the morning Love-Feast, pointed out another woman to me as "so worldly," and " not living up to her profession at all." I did not know the other woman, and it was perfectly unnecessary, and very unkind. How could I believe in my friend's "perfect love" after that? I do want to see it lived, as well as to hear it talked—then I should feel courage to go on. But so long as I see that Holiness professors do not love each other, how can I think there is anything in Holiness but mere talk?

Suppose she had been able to say "our Hall" instead of "our Church," dear comrade, would your conscience, as you read her words, have arraigned you as among those stumbling blocks in the King's way whose words of love in the Meeting turn to words of spite outside, and bring the poor, struggling half-hearts to an utter standstill?

"Out of the abundance of the heart the mouth speaketh," and where God has purified all the affections, and filled the heart with His Spirit, the words that come out will be like those of Jesus, and that likeness will prove the speaker to be His disciple.

Love That Descends

Jesus, knowing that the Father had given all things into His hands, and that He was come from God, and went to God . . . began to wash the disciples' feet, and to wipe them with the towel wherewith He was

> *girded. . . . For I have given you an example. That yet*
> *should do as I have done to you* (John 13:3, 5, 15).

The mind staggers when it tries to grasp the distance from that tremendous height where all things were given into the hands of Jesus by God from whom He came, down to the valley bottom where He could wash His servants' feet! But if we can only stand bewildered before the amazing condescension of God, we can turn with refreshment and joy to the fact that it was love which descended to that immeasurable depth, and love we can understand because we feel it in our own hearts. "To know the love of Christ, that passeth knowledge," that is the inexplicable experience which must be possessed to be apprehended, since it transcends expression.

Jesus realized fully all that He was in Divine Essence, and yet He not only came to our level, but put Himself below it, in service, to show us how love must be manifested. Has your love produced the service spirit in you, my comrade? If not, if it is satisfied always to take in and never to give out; if it lets you rest in your own Salvation, uncaring for the Salvation of others; if it likes better to be served than to help; if it counts anything but conscience too dear to part with to please or serve its neighbor—it does not bear the stamp of Jesus, and needs perfecting in order that you may do as He did.

Whatever earthly height you may have to descend from, whatever earthly garments you may have to lay aside, the love of Jesus brightly burning in your heart will make any descent, any sacrifice easy, pleasant, and even joyous. A woman once said to me, "I should like to help fallen women, and it often seems as if there were things I might do, but my social position prevents me!"

She made me shiver. In a few short years, at most, the great church bells next door would clang out her parting knell, and her position before the Judgment Bar was the thing I had to consider. There was but a tiny step downward from her blue and gold drawing room to the street where those poor souls were dying like moths, and she would not take it, though Jesus had descended those unthinkable heights for her! She had no Divine love in her—her feet had never been washed by Jesus, or she must have followed after lost souls as He did. Christ-washed feet are the ones which are "beautiful upon the mountains, bringing glad tidings." Christ-washed feet always follow the Savior's path, and the heart filled with His love which they carry forgets when it came and whither it goes, *because* Jesus remembered, and yet served!

> My Savior, how shall I proclaim,
>   How pay the mighty debt I owe?
> Let all I have, and all I am,
>   Ceaseless to all Thy Glory show.
>
> Too much to Thee I cannot give;
>   Too much I cannot do for Thee;
> Let all Thy love and all Thy grief
>   Graven on my heart for ever be.

Imperfect Faith

I have prayed for thee, that thy faith fail not (Luke 22::32).

Peter was in sore need of his Savior's help at this stage of his Christian life. He had plenty of pride and ambition left; impulse ruled him; he was fickle and high-tempered—not a meek or model Christian at all. But his Master, who loved him with all the tender heart of God, looked beneath these defects to their root and spring—his weak, imperfect faith, and prayed for that.

Peter trusted God perfectly at last, on the day of Pentecost, and then the perfect love which resulted from entire trust removed all his heart blemishes, and left him clean in the sight of God.

That mighty faith on me bestow
That cannot ask in vain;
Which holds and will not let Thee go,
Till I my suit obtain.

Till Thou into my soul inspire
The perfect love unknown,
And tell my infinite desire,
Whate'er Thou wilt, be done.

But is it possible that I
Should live and sin no more?
Lord, if on Thee I dare rely,,
The faith shall bring the power.

On me that faith Divine bestow
Which doth the mountain move;
And all my spotless life shall show
The omnipotence of love.

Confess It Out

If ye love Me, keep my commandments (John 14:15).

These love texts, running all through our Lord's last talk with His disciples, are like a golden wedding ring given by God to His Church. They begin with our love to Him, reach out around all His people in all time, and come back to Him again, binding love to God and love to man in one perfectly cohering circle.

"If ye love Me!" Ah, Lord, we love Thee; we have chosen Thee before all the world; we have entered into covenant with Thee; we have taken Thy name upon us; we have no business in life except to obey Thee.

Then, "keep My commandments." And our Master sums them all up in one short verse: "This is My commandment, that ye love one another, as I have loved you."

But Thou art God! How shall a frail, erring, human heart, whose nature is evil, love like Thee, whose very essence is pure, perfect, glowing love? Can a man love like God, any more than He can make worlds as God did? True, he cannot; we admit it. But God in him can do it. "Christ, the power of God and the wisdom of God," taking full possession of body, soul, and spirit, can do it. Why a child can see the steps, they rise so easily and simply. A child must must understand that the Omnipotent God, if allowed full, unhindered sway with a human will, can make it operate righteously; can make human emotions always true and pure and right. The only really puzzling question must be the practical one, "How shall He get possession? How am I to be rid of this opposing, distracting self which hinders His abiding, and often forces the withdrawal of His Spirit against my will and intention?

Confess it out. If your will is really surrendered to God, the "old man" must be hunted out of hiding places by exposure—confession. He lives in the dark, and light kills him. John Wesley's "Holiness bands" were instituted for the sole purpose of confessing the carnal nature to its death. When we confess our past transgressions they are forgiven; when we confess the manifestations of our iniquity—the tendency to sin in us—God can blot it out, if we trust in Him to do it. This is a most practical point, but it is one too much neglected in theoretical teaching. Look, however, at your Penitent-Form or altar work. You find that souls seldom "get anywhere" till they tell out the thing that they need to give up. Then light dawns; then, they can take the next step.

I read the other day the touching experience of a converted African heathen, told with and almost infantile simplicity. The lad had thought he had a good experience, but noticed that when he saw a banana on the table he felt covetous and greedy about it; that there were two of his teachers whom he did not like, and he felt slight resentments towards different ones. So he confessed out these remnants, these odds and ends of self left littering his heart, until God took them away, and he was able to love unselfishly, perfectly, aboundingly.

I had to confess out chattering and chafing, just as that poor Congo boy did his hindrances, to people who thought my difficulties as laughable as, perhaps, you think his banana coveting. But when it was confessed, God blessed me, and comforted me, and gave me such a positive assurance of His pleasure with me as I would not have given back for ages of fun. "People can't believe for Holiness till they confess out," spoke the Congo lad out of his own joyful, victorious experience.

Many other have had to pass through this infinitesimal sieve of confession; but the process has left them clear and clean in the light itself. Then when confession has done its work, just "open the door" of faith, and Jesus has said, "We will come unto him, and make Our abode with him."

Your Legacy

Peace I leave with you; My peace I give unto you
(John 14:27).

Comrade, have you secured your legacy—the peace which cannot be shaken or destroyed, which Jesus left for you?

Why not? You would not hesitate to secure a gift of dollars or diamonds which was yours by bequest. Why, then, leave unpossessed something which will be of more use to you, will bring you more happiness today, and will be still blessing you when the world shall be no more?

It is not a little thing that God has willed you here—"peace like a river, enriching and making fruitful all the land where you dwell; "peace which passeth all understanding." Keep your soul strong under trials that seem inexplicable. And when the storm demons seem let loose upon the soul, and the waves rise mountains high, even then this peace remains unbroken. It is left for you, and there is nothing that can hinder you taking possession of it if you will.

Lying Spirits

When He, the Spirit of truth, is come, He will guide
you into all truth. . . . He shall glorify Me. . . . All
things that the Father hath are mine; therefore said I,
that He shall take of Mine, and shall show it unto
you (John 16:13-15).

The After Meeting was drawing to a close, when I went to speak to a young man, not very intelligent looking, who sat near the front. We could not seem to reach any point in our talk, but presently the young man straightened up from his slouching attitude, and declared himself, "I don't believe much I've heard. I'm a Spiritualist; and, what's more, I'm a medium.

"You really think that departed spirits communicate with you?"

"I know they do," with profound conviction; "they write on my slate!"

"Do you think they come from God or from the Devil?"

"From God. They tell me I'm going to Heaven."

"But you are still in sin, and God says in His word that you cannot go to Heaven unless you are born again. What do your supposed spirits say about Jesus?"

"That He was a man, same as I am."

"But God's Spirit, the Spirit of truth, is to glorify Jesus, and testify to His Divinity. And any spirit which contradicts the Holy Spirit must be of the Devil."

The poor lad had been an ardent Sunday School scholar and church member while he lived with his mother in the south, but three months' listening to "lying spirits" up in this northern city had turned him into a hardened sceptic. He never prayed, had no use for his Bible, and cared for nothing except to escape Hell without cost.

Comrade, not all the "lying spirits" exhibit themselves cheaply at twenty-five cents a head, and scrawl weak platitudes on slates. Some are largely occupied in writing books, possibly of most lofty moral tone or dealing entirely with spiritual topics, or explaining a generous higher criticism. But you need only apply the test of these words of Jesus to them to discover their origin of evil, however plausible, reasonable, and friendly to orthodoxy they may appear.

Do they "glorify" Jesus, or do they reduce Him to the level of Buddha, and other poor gods? Do they testify of

Him as "the Lamb of God, which taketh away the sin of
the world," or do they leave you without an atonement for
your past, its guilt and burden for ever to remain upon your
helpless soul? Do they guide you into all truth as He
revealed and taught it, or do they guide you into a maze of
philosophical speculation and poetical wonderment, which
leaves you at last nothing but dreams, and practically takes
from you the Book which has revealed God to you? Do they
"reprove the world of sin," or do they excuse, cover, and
defend sin, trusting vaguely to the false "mercy" of a God
who by their theory condones sin instead of abolishing it?

If they differ in these points from the Spirit whom Jesus
promised to us, and who made His glorious advent into
three thousand happy hearts on the day of Pentecost, then,
whether they scrawl on slates or send out their lies in
much-praised books, have nothing to do with them. Shun
them like vipers, like subtle, deadliest poisons, like the
very snare and sword of the Devil himself.

"Lead us not into temptation, but deliver us from evil."

"Consider Him"

*Jesus, therefore, knowing all things that should come
upon Him, went forth* (John 18:4).

We often look back along our own little thorn-set path-
way, and say, "If I had known it all beforehand, I could not
have walked this road; but God mercifully hid it from me.
He led me step by step, gave me hourly grace, held fast my
hand all the way, and so I have come." And then we thank
Him that the same helping veil of ignorance hides all the
future way from us, so that we have only to love, and trust,

and set the next footstep where He shows us, and where His own makes a companion print as we go.

But Jesus, as His feet drew near Calvary, knew beforehand its unspeakable terrors. He know that He would go out from that quiet garden to hours of hatred and scorning, "exceedingly filled with contempt," which should only end on the awful cross.

He knew each pang for His body, each crushing gibe and reproach for His heart—knew beforehand the weight of inworking human depravity to be poured out upon His spotless, innocent soul—knew the utter loneliness, the sting of desertion, the failure of all human love and gratitude—heard the last cries of His suffering flesh with its generation for ever undeclared (Isa. 53:8), its every human feeling, hope, and longing crushed out of existence—heard the taunts of men and devils, defaming, belying, blasting Him, and yet "He went forth." How could He! How could He!

"Jesus, the beginner and finisher of our faith, for the joy that was set before Him, endured the cross, despising the shame."

But what joy could be seen across the immense stretch of horror and desolation between Him and the far side of the cross? The joy of having His human will entirely lost in the Divine will—the joy of the Salvation for others which must result from the sacrifice of self—these lasting joys He saw by faith. That faith is "the faith of the Son of God," by which Paul declares that he lived, and by which his wonderful sacrifices—still working out Salvation for God's Church, still bearing great fruit of joy in two worlds—were made.

This is the joy of which Jesus spoke before to His disciples,"These things have I spoken unto you, that My joy may remain in you, and that your joy may be full." Full—brimming, satisfying, Heaven-like joy—the very joy of God!

Comrade, there is no other joy. Its source is the perfect absolute submission to God which brings us to and keeps us in His immediate presence, where, as David tells us, "is fullness of joy."

Perhaps you know already where your hill of Calvary rises towards Heaven, and you see the somber cross awaiting you at its foot. But you lack power to go forth—your flesh and your heart fail you, and God is not your strength for this, nor your portion for any such intolerable place. Then, "consider Him who endured such contradiction of sinners against Himself." Consider Him who endures this contradiction of your will to His tender, loving, and (if you could but know it) infinitely beautiful will for you until you can believe His love, trust His providence—submit and obey. You have long dwelt on your own sorrows—the hardness of your lot, as compared with the light and ornamental cross of other Christians—now, "consider Jesus."

You do *not* know what is before you. God does. The Devil says there is only pain and loss, there is only useless toil and sacrifice; but God calls you by this very way to His presence, to union with Him, to radiant light, to a joy that *can* endure the cross.

Jesus went forth for you, knowing what you never can know; went forth to bear all the flesh cannot endure, to take once for all, every real bitter from the cup of life, and leave there only the living water. Drink of His cup, and while it brings death to self, you will find, as you drink, the shadows fleeing the fair day breaking, and a new earth begun for you.

Not Power, But God

And they were all filled with the Holy Ghost (Acts 1:4).

Because "the cloven tongues, like as of fire," settled upon each of these believers, we are apt to fix our minds on these visible manifestations of the Spirit, and accept the mistaken idea that being filled with the Holy Ghost is an extraordinary and difficult state to attain; that it must always be accompanied by visions and miracles. In reality, it is, though supernatural, the normal, healthy state of the soul, ordained by God for every one of His true children.

Think for a minute. The Holy Ghost is the Spirit of God. By His own statement, "God is love"; but the necessity of the case that love is perfect; so, to be filled with the Holy Ghost is to be filled with perfect love.

"I struggled and wrestled to win it," sings a soul who has found out the better way. But those hundred and twenty did not wrestle or struggle. It is true that they "continued in prayer and supplication." But they had come back from Bethany "with great joy," although Jesus had gone up out of their sight. They believed now, and faith *is* continually "praising and blessing God." They really expected the promise of the Father for which they were tarrying. They got what they expected *by seeking God,* and no one since their time has obtained the fulfillment of that promise in any other way.

We are not to seek power, but God. God has no "power to let," like the property owners along rivers and water-sides. It was never known that He gave His power away. But He comes in Himself to the surrendered, believing human heart, and abiding there, exerts His power in us and through us.

Do not pray for power, comrade; the command is, "Seek

115

you Me," not "Seek ye power." Pray instead that God will cleanse His temple, and abide in it for ever. Then, when you believe His promise in this very thing, it will be done. His glory will fill your poor temple, and you will not be able at times to distinguish His presence there from His presence in the greater, higher Heaven where you used to think He alone dwelt.

When the Holy Spirit once comes to abide in you, you will "receive power" as the disciples did (verse 8), to "witness unto Jesus" wherever you may be—in your native place, in your home country, among enemies, among strangers, among the "uttermost" heathen.

Long before Jesus had told His disciples that when the Comforter came, He would testify of Him, and He repeated it just before He ascended into Heaven. Over and over again we are told that Jesus is the possessor of all Divine power, and that by the Person of the Holy Spirit He communicates Himself to you and me. That indwelling alone must constitute our power.

The Source of Joy

Thou shalt make me full of joy with Thy countenance
(Acts 2:28).

Comrade, what is the source of your joy? David, and his great Son after him, found the sum of all their happiness in the countenance—the sought for, realized, blissful presence— of God.

All things else must fail us; "human hearts and looks deceive us"; at least, in the sense that they never can fulfil our unreasonable expectations and demands. The experiences and circumstances from which we most certainly look for joy are surest to disappoint us. But it is possible to love Him so entirely that the mere thought of His presence fills one's heart to overflowing with joy. To look by faith into the face of God gives the sanctified soul a happiness that nothing else can.

How does one find this joy-giving countenance of God?

Paul tells the Corinthians, "We all with unveiled [Rotherham's translation] face behold as in a glass the glory of the Lord"; we see Him in His word and works where He is mirrored and reflected forth. Look at the third chapter of that second letter to the Church at Corinth. "Beholding in the glass," that reflection is nothing else than "reading of the Old Testament" about Him: and we find the explanation, the fulfillment, the perfect complement of that Old Testament in the New.

But it is useless to look for God in His word with the veil of doubt upon the heart; it is faith alone which can apprehend Him. "Nevertheless, when your heart shall turn to the Lord, the veil shall be taken away." I have seen blank infidelity approach that word with a real hunger for the unknown, discredited God, honestly wishing to learn the truth, and find Him there—and it has done so. God is revealed there to the soul that unreservedly seeks for Him, and the one who finds Him finds fullness of joy.

"What were you doing up so frightfully early?" I heard a Soldier ask this morning.

"Reading my Bible, and praying, and having a good time generally," was the answer. No reason for doing it, except for pleasure; but the face that had seen God's countenance since early down was radiant with joy.

> With us no melancholy void,
> No period lingers unemployed,

Or unimproved below;
Our weariness of life is gone,
Who live to serve our God alone
And only Thee to know.

The World's Misery and You

God, having raised up His Son Jesus, sent Him to
bless you, in turning away every one of you from his
iniquities (Acts 3:26).

"I see so much misery and sin about me everywhere,
that I sometimes doubt if there is any such thing as
Salvation."

That was all I heard her say—a young mother giving her
baby some breaths of sea air in the breezy pavilion where I
was writing. The baby cooed at her cheerfully, and she
picked it up, and went away from the questioning
Salvationist on the other side. She would not even stop to
hear the beautiful, tender message, and learn how God
would take away the "sin and misery" from her own heart,
and at least lessen by so much, the sum of both in her
world.

Reader, if the world's wretchedness weighs upon your
heart, look at the message God sends in this verse. He has
sent Jesus "to bless you." The earth's wide curse is not
God's, not of His devising, nor His inflicting. He has
"thoughts of good, and not of evil concerning you; hands of
love stretching out to you always; His very Spirit is named
the Comforter, and His own name of "Father" suggests no
action that is not for your good.

But God's love is not a helpless feeling, like ours for
those who are dear to us; His blessing is a practical one,

and brings with it the remedy for our woes. He will turn you away from your iniquity, and you shall "remember your misery as waters that pass away."

Look within your heart, the seat and center of all your iniquity. It is there that God will meet you, there that He will search out your sins, and show you your wickedness as it is in His sight; there that He will judge you, and, if you will repent, forgive you, cleanse you, and make you altogether a new creature.

Look within, I say; seek God in the temple of your being, and there you will find Him, seeking you. God has been waiting at the door of your heart ever since your earliest consciousness of right and wrong. "Behold, I stand at the door, and knock." Do not waste anymore time looking at the wickedness and consequent wretchedness around you, when the same thing, in perhaps a different degree, is within you. You are unlike Jesus—that is your sole trouble, and the sum of all your sin. You must be "renewed in the spirit of your mind"—born again by the Spirit of God into the moral likeness of Jesus. This is the solution of the problem of earthly badness and sadness. Experience this new birth for yourself, and then pass on your knowledge of others.

> Lo, in the silent night a child of God is born,
> And all is brought again that e'er was lost or lorn
> Would by thy soul, O man, become a silent night,
> God would be born in thee, and set all things aright.

Prayer That Prevails

And now, Lord, behold their threatenings: and grant unto Thy servants, that with all boldness they may speak Thy word (Acts 4:29).

Here is an instance of effectual praying written out for our imitation. The Apostles have been stringently threatened about preaching Jesus, and they quite believed that evil consequences would follow if they continued. Yet being constrained to preach the Gospel, they took measures on their knees to do the right thing in the right way.

First, they considered the One who had given them orders; the extent of His rule and of His power. The words told us are few, but what magnificent vistas they open up before our souls of the kingdom and sovereignty of our God! The Apostles, maybe, spent long time over this part of their praying, and what confidence it would give them to go on and ask great things!

Then they acknowledged to God that all their past, seemingly adverse circumstances were ordered by Him; and, more than that, were foretold by Him; and so they accepted them with a matter-of-factness which implied the reverse of grumbling, or even questioning. There is no moaning in this prayer.

And last, they laid their present case before their Savior, and asked, not that He would make things easier or pleasanter, but only that He would give grace equal to the necessity—would give them Divine power to obey orders, regardless of consequences. The prayer is all in the Spirit, and according to the will of God; it runs parallel, throughout its whole length, with the prayers and teaching of Jesus; it seeks His Kingdom and glory only, and ignores self entirely.

Such a prayer must prevail with God; it needed an immediate answer, and we read that the Holy Spirit came to them in outpouring fullness, and they "spake the word of God with boldness."

An Open Secret

But we will give ourselves continually to prayer, and ministry of the word (Acts 6:4).

No one will deny that the disciples were eminently successful Officers. They not only made grand openings, but their Corps stood, and their Soldiers were of the sort who went joyously to death for Jesus' sake. It was not, however, by virtue of an excellent education that they succeeded, for people who heard them speak a very little easily discovered that they were "unlearned and ignorant men." But just as they were almost always with Jesus in bodily presence while He was with them, so they stayed with Him afterwards, "continually in prayer," and His presence and power were felt wherever they spoke.

The modern Apostles are not different. We have all seen towns moved, cities stirred, souls swept into the Kingdom in masses, by personally insignificant, almost wholly uneducated striplings. The files of our Army papers are full of such records, the names of these lads and lasses are plain to see among them, and thousands have blessed God for their work. But both in the time of the early Church, and in all the recorded days of The Salvation Army, the work was done by disciples who lived on their knees. It is an open secret, both in the Bible and among us.

Financial Difficulties

Then the twelve called the multitude of the disciples unto them, and said, It is not reason that we should leave the word of God, and serve tables. Wherefore,

> *brethren, look ye out among you seven men of honest*
> *report, full of the Holy Ghost and wisdom, whom we*
> *may appoint over this business* (Acts 6:2, 3).

There was a call for businessmen in the early Church; the prototype of the Social Wing had grown up among the "multiplied disciples," and Officers were wanted.

"Any one" would not do for this work. The Apostles specified that these new Social stewards were to be "men of honest report"—established Converts, not Recruits of yesterday. Then it was required that they be "full of the Holy Ghost"; for supernatural wisdom is needed to raise interest without principal, supplies without a base, and much of something from apparently nothing. The Church flourished as a whole, when seven Officers of this description, headed by one especially "full of faith and of the Holy Ghost," got to work; we read that the word of God increased, the number of disciples was greatly multiplied, and even a "great company" of the priests converted.

Now what plain, practical, Bible rule for conducting financial operations in any religious organization can be deduced from this little bit of church history?

It can be no other than the one laid down by their Master a few years before: "Seek ye first the kingdom of Heaven, and all these things shall be added unto you." When one remembers that "the kingdom of God is within you," and that it is "not meat and drink, but righteousness, and peace, and joy in the Holy Ghost," this seems a roundabout way of managing secular affairs. Especially as "seeking the kingdom" is not here, as it is sometimes, to be interpreted as seeking the Salvation of other souls. It is seeking first to establish, and then to continue, a perfect harmony and communion of the individual soul with God. Once this is done, the Salvation of others works out naturally and easily from your own, for the Kingdom of Heaven is like plants, it grows, spreads, multiples. Let the Kingdom of God reign in you, and you will conquer others for the King.

But now to come to your financial burden, in Corps, church, or mission. The man who "seeks the kingdom" in the wholehearted way which God requires, is on dealing terms with the One to whom the earth itself belongs, in whose hands are the "hearts of the kings of the earth"; who rules the seasons, the crops, and all things. This man can plead the promise "God shall supply all your need," and have it literally and liberally fulfilled to him. He has fulfilled the condition of "seeking first the kingdom," and the promise of "all these things" is made good to him.

Let God Fulfil in You All His Good Pleasure

Who, when they were come down, prayed for them, that they might receive the Holy Ghost: for as yet He was fallen upon none of them: only they were baptized in the name of the Lord Jesus (Acts 8:15, 16).

"How long do you have to wait after you're converted before you get the Holy Ghost?" asked an unconverted lad of me after a late "Free-and-Easy" Meeting. "Because all the folks on the platform haven't got it. Why don't they all get it?"

"Some of them are very recently converted," I told him.

"Yes, but some of 'em have been converted as long as I've been here. Why don't they go on? Don't they know they can't go to Heaven till they're sanctified any more than I can? They ought to go ahead. It's in the Bible, plain

as A B C. Why don't every Christian get filled with the
Holy Ghost? That's what I mean to do when I once start."

The boy had a Bible, and maybe he had been reading
about this very prayer of the Apostles. At any rate, his
theology was sound and Scriptural; the "second blessing" is
taught here as plainly as language can express it.

These Samaritans must have given evidence of saving
faith, or the careful Philip would not have "baptized them
in the name of the Lord Jesus, " for the church leaders of
those days were not anxious for nominal members, but
weighed their personal testimony to conversion well before
accepting them (Acts 10:45, and 15:15). And after their conversion—sometimes very long after, as in the days of
Cornelius—by surrender and faith they "received the Holy
Ghost"; in equivalent Bible terms they became "sanctified," "holy," received "clean hearts."

What was the difference in these people before the Holy
Ghost fell on them and after? We know from Scripture that
they "spoke with other tongues." So people who become
sanctified do now. Their words have weight and power far
beyond what is merely natural; they can "prophesy" (testify) of the Salvation of God, and tell of all His wondrous
works in a way impossible to them when only converted.

I recently heard a man, genuinely converted, denying the
possibility of Holiness to another who claimed the possession of a clean heart. He brought against the other "railing
accusations," which God's saints in Heaven or earth do not
allow themselves; his eyes flashed fire in the heat of his
vexation, while the other's beamed only love; if a deaf man
had watched the two, he must clearly have seen the great
and painful difference. Yet when the heat of the disputant
had cooled, and his ordinary spirit was allowed to rule, he
appeared again a humble, loving Christian.

There are two spirits in a justified man; there is only the
one Spirit, even the Holy Ghost Himself, actuating the
sanctified man, and that is always the spirit of love.

St. John propounded the doctrine of this second work of Holiness as distinctly as ever Wesley or William Booth have done, when he wrote, "But this spake He of the Spirit which they that believe on Him should receive; for the Holy Ghost was not yet given; because that Jesus was not yet glorified."

Jesus proclaimed it unmistakably when He said, "I will pray the Father, and He will give you another Comforter, that He may abide with you for ever: even the Spirit of Truth: whom the world cannot receive, because it seeth Him not, neither knoweth Him: but ye know Him, for He dwelleth with you, and shall be in you."

The disciples were already converted—they "knew the Spirit"; again, the phrase, "He dwelleth with you," indicated the first work, of conversion, in them; the statement, "He shall be in you," describes the continuous abiding of the Spirit in the second work of sanctification.

Besides the Scripture teaching of this second work, we have the strong, unmistakable testimony of hundreds of living Christians to the fact in their own experience.

But without argument, comrade, does the Holy Spirit abide in your heart? Does He continue there from day to day, neither grieved by anger, pride, or unbelief, or driven away, however briefly, by any sin? If not, why will you not claim for yourself the promise of Jesus that He shall abide with you for ever?

Love is the law of spiritual life, and whatever is contradictory to love in you imperils your spiritual life, and must weaken and retard your spiritual development. More than that, the very sinners whom you wish to help are hindered by you; your words fall idly on their ears when they know by your face, testimony, and life, that you have not received all that God has for you, and have not fulfilled His will for you, "even your sanctification."

Do not be a grief to Jesus and a stumbling block to His wandering sheep any longer, but let Him fulfil in you "all the good pleasure of His goodness, and the work of faith with power."

"A Chosen Vessel"

But the Lord said unto him, Go thy way; for he is a chosen vessel unto Me, to bear My name before the Gentiles, and kings, and the children of Israel. For I will show him how great things he must suffer for My name's sake (Acts 9:15, 16).

The man who desires an easy, thornless path through life, must never love. The woman who fears care and trouble, and a life-long succession of trials, would better put away at the beginning every tender affection, for each one will mean sacrifice and consequent suffering; and the more unselfish the passion, the keener will grow its pangs. The love of country, of friends, of family, of God, bring with them, from any self-seeking standpoint, a suffering through abnegation, proportioned to the love. But who would live without loving? Better have been created a piece of flint or granite than not to spend oneself in loving people, in loving and adoring God.

Paul, then, had to suffer great things, but ah! the compensations hidden in the meaning of these words, "a chosen vessel unto Me," and "for My name's sake"! The poor "earthen vessel" was purified from every stain, and constantly filled to overflowing by the satisfying joy-bringing love of God. And as Jesus chose Paul, so, in turn, did Paul choose Jesus to be his Lord, on whom to pour out the overmastering, consuming love of his life. Paul was upborn from every form of suffering by this always-swelling tide of

Divine love pouring through his whole being, and bearing him constantly towards its Source.

Later on, when he was going towards Jerusalem, and knew through the Spirit that bonds and afflictions were awaiting him there, he told his comrades, "None of these things move me, neither count I my life dear unto myself, so that I might finish my course with joy."

Paul suffered all that a mortal well can, and yet the dominant chord in all his recorded experiences is a harmony of joy, peace, and blessedness. All through his stormy "course" the joy outweighed the suffering, covered it out of sight, reduced it to the merest memory.

Comrade, have you such love for Jesus that the physical and mental part of you, which will be capable of suffering as long as you are in the body, are no longer "dear to you," because the inner life, the real life, is one of such constant joy in Him? Paul's experience is not one peculiar to his temperament, or his way of looking at things; joy is the fruit of the Spirit; and Paul abounded in that most precious fruit because the Spirit was given to him, as it will be to you, if you choose, "without measure."

"Sorrowful" you may be, or heavy through manifold temptations, but "always rejoicing" you ought to be. Get the love which will make you so, comrade. God will take out of you everything which is contrary to love—all the malice, indolence, petulance, impatience, pride, ill-temper—the whole catalog of evils which go to make up the carnal mind—and fill you with His Spirit. What else can fit you for Heaven? What else gives you fitness for your life and work in this world?

On Knowing the Will of God

*And he said, The God of our fathers hath chosen thee,
that thou shouldest know His will, and see that Just
One, and shouldest hear the voice of His mouth* (Acts
22:14).

I meet people everywhere who are greatly concerned
about their work for God. They feel absolutely certain that
He has a work for them, and yet they cannot find out what
it is; or, if they get an inkling of its nature, they have not
an idea how to set about it. To discover this is, and should
be, the great concern of their lives.

There was, surely, never a more successful Christian
worker than Paul, or one who more exactly and fully carried out God's will for him. And here is Paul's plan of work
plainly marked out for him beforehand, by God Himself;
and as surely as Paul followed out this plan, so surely no
man since his day has succeeded before God in any other
way than that of God's ordering.

Paul's work had to begin where yours must—within, and
not without. "To know the will of God" is the first work
for a Convert to undertake. God has saved you, I suppose,
since you want to work for Him. That is assuredly a part of
His will for you, for He is "not willing that any should perish, but that all should come to repentance." And the next
step in His will for you is this, "even your sanctification."

After these things are accomplished in you, God will
reveal His will to you, unmistakably, clearly; but to the end
of your days, your first business as a Christian worker will
be, to find out the will of God that you may fulfil it. This
involves the continual seeking of His face, in prayer, in His
word, and in His works, for the mind of God is only
revealed to that faith which perpetually seeks Him. Oh, the
insatiable longing of a living faith for God! It is always

being satisfied, yet always craving; always finding, yet always seeking. Its mysterious paradox can only be understood by those who possess it.

"But," cries a weak soul, " I have not faith. These things are not real to me. How can I 'have faith' of myself?"

You *have* a degree of faith. Use what faith you have. Find promises in the Book that you can claim, and plead them with God till your faith holds firm. The deep things of God are revealed "from faith to faith"; that is, faith mounts like a ladder; you must take one step, and it then becomes possible for you to take the next. Another free translation is, "You must use what you have before you will get any more." Is not that true of a baby's strength? Your soul will grow faster than a baby's body, but it is by the same means—food and exercise—always feeding on the Word and the Spirit, and *using* the strength you get thereby.

Give up the idea of doing anything for God until you know His will." You think that will make you wait too long in silence and idleness? Oh, no. God made me testify in a Meeting within an hour after He converted me, and the testifying was most distinctly doing His will, and was very contrary indeed to my own. Then, He set me to work for souls within a week; but always, early and late, He kept me seeking His face, praying incessantly, and digging with might and main into my little textbook, making me know His will. And I say with deep conviction, that the knowledge of His will in my inmost soul, and the total surrender of my will to His, always went ahead of any attempt at work.

God chose Paul to "see the Just One," and "hear the voice of His mouth." So He chooses you. It does not mean seeing visions or hearing dream voices. When Jesus is revealed in you as He was in Paul, you will be more absolutely sure of His personality, His identity, His love, than you are of that of any human being. Doubt cries out, "Oh, that I could see Jesus, that I could be *sure!*" Faith answers, in assurance, "I know whom I have believed." "Hereby know we that we dwell in Him, and He in us, because He hath given us of His Spirit."

The pure in heart see God. Let God by faith cleanse your heart from all sin, and fill it with His Spirit, and your unveiled spiritual eyes will behold Him, your unstopped ears will hear His voice. "He calleth His own sheep by name," said Jesus, ". . . for they know His voice."

Then, when you have a personal knowledge of your Lord, and are daily learning His will, "thou shalt be His witness unto all men of what thou hast seen and heard." Did you ever know any good to come of preaching which had not a genuine experience and definite testimony to back it? No! Neither will any good come of your "work" until you are made a worker in God's way—until you "know His will," and see and hear Him; not only through other people, but directly, for yourself.

Joy in the Cross

And the night following the Lord stood by him, and said, Be of good cheer, Paul; for as thou hast testified of Me in Jerusalem, so must thou bear witness also at Rome (Acts 23:11).

Paul's experience in testifying to the Lord Jesus in Jerusalem could be no means be called pleasant or comfortable. "They went about to slay him" the first time he did it; and on the second occasion he was beaten, bound, came near to being pulled to pieces, and finally was imprisoned. And yet his Lord held out the prospect of bearing witness for Him in the same way at Rome as matter for "good cheer."

And not without reason. Paul had known before he went to Jerusalem that bonds and afflictions awaited him, but he had answered that they mattered nothing, nor did his life itself count for anything, so that he might finish his course "with joy." He seems to have found in the "fellowship of Christ's sufferings" the highest type of earthly joy. The flesh and the Spirit are "contrary the one to the other" now, as they were when Paul wrote to the Galatians; but as then, so now when the flesh is wholly subdued to the Spirit, the soul is capable and conscious of joys which are unknown to sense, joys so keen and subtle that they cannot be defined by words, which it is not possible for man to utter."

You say that only Paul had this experience. No. God's riches are for all His children, and they have possessed them, in all ages, in proportion to their faith. See how Madame Guyon pours out, like a soaring lark, that rapture to which Paul and David also gave utterance:

> Adieu! ye vain delights of earth,
> Insipid sports, and childish mirth,
>   I taste no sweets in you!
> Unknown delights are in the cross,
> All joy beside, to me is dross;
>   And Jesus thought so too.

It was said of the dying Fletcher, by his wife: "He seemed to enjoyed the cross; according to a word which he used often to repeat, 'We are to seek a perfect conformity to the will of God, and have Him to give us pleasure or pain, as it seemeth Him good.'"

Why is it that the keenest rapture which the Christian knows, does not come to him in the rapid, joyous Public Meeting, where even the outsider can see that Salvation is a happy and glorious possession? Because God is the Source of all joy, the Fountainhead of all bliss, and the soul comes to the fullest knowledge of Him in silent communion, without sights, sounds, or any form of expression to hamper its perception of Him. "Too deep for words," too ethereal for vision, eluding even thought, is the impression of God's Spirit on the waiting soul: and where cross or loss separate us farthest from the world and its once-prized pleasures, the more open are we to that Spirit, the more readily do we "plunge in the Godhead's deepest sea."

On Testimony

I have appeared unto thee for this purpose, to make thee a minister and a witness (Acts 26:16).

"I don't like to sing, 'Oh, how I love Jesus!' I'd rather sing, 'I am so glad that Jesus loves me.' I think we ought to talk less of the way we feel, and more of the way God feels."

The speaker was a Christian worker, of at least fifteen years' standing; he had just been engaged, alas! in a violent attack on heart purity, and this was his final shot.

But God's purpose, as He here tells Paul, is, that men shall witness to what He had done in them. God does not change; He is eternally the same, and a sinner can sing of His love with as much truthfulness as a saint. But when by His miracle-working Spirit He turns our stony, indifferent hearts to love Him, what a change in us! Ah! there is a topic to sing and talk about, on which a sinners' lips must not remain closed. If we held our peace about this wonderful change, the stones should cry out against us.

Paul kept the command to testify. There came many to

him in his lodging at Rome, "to whom he expounded and testified of the kingdom of God." He was not satisfied simply to tell the people what God was *able to do*, but made a helpful lesson of his own experience by relating what God *had done* in him. Testify to the possession of what you teach others they ought to have, and give God all the glory.

Wayside Ministries

I long to see you, that I may impart unto you some spiritual gifts, to the end ye may be established (Rom. 1:11).

Long ago, three of us, spiritual babies, used to haunt Headquarters, in Queen Victoria Street, to get help for our souls. We went there at all hours when it was open, and under all pretexts; but whether we loitered in the little front shop looking at the photographs and books, went to the top floor to try on a bonnet, dived into the basement for scissors and pamphlets, or even mounted to look over London from the roof, the man or woman in uniform who showed us about was always trying to impart some spiritual gift to us, and slowly, piecemeal it may be, all were helping to get us established in God.

Today I am profoundly grateful to them all that they did not waste those precious hours in doctrinal discussions, in light and foolish talk, in unprofitable joking, or even, so far as I can remember, in explaining The Salvation Army to my ignorant mind. They fed my soul, and helped me to know Jesus better, and always sent me away better and wiser than when I came.

It ought to be like that everywhere on this heavenly way, beloved fellow traveler. It is beautifully possible for each happy possessor of God's Salvation to help not only sinners but other Christians to a deeper knowledge of Jesus. We need not be older, or wiser, or better than others in order to help their souls; we need only to be filled with God's Spirit.

"Let no man despise thy youth," wrote Paul to young Timothy, "but be thou an example to the believer, in word, in faith, in conversation." Paul is very explicit on the matter of Timothy's talk; he is to "avoid profane [worldly] and vain babblings [light chatter]"—explaining in the next letter, as he reiterates his charge, that they "will increase unto more ungodliness."

So they will. Have you not found it so? Have you never separated from a Christian friend, after some minutes' exchange of polite nothings, with a feeling of dissatisfaction, of hunger, almost of self-condemnation? Timothy was not to argue, not to chatter; he was to give himself to reading, and to exhortation, if he needed to express himself.

"Let all things be done unto edifying"—building up. Are all your social meetings and doings with a view to building up the Kingdom of God? It is to be hoped that, in all Army centers, weak souls are built up and strengthened in God. and no doubt you see how fit it is that it should be so. But how about your home, your office, your places of resort? Does God's business, God's talk, God's invisible work, have the first consideration, the best chance, there? God will so bless you as it does.

> Our friendship sanctify and guide;
> Unmixed with selfishness and pride,
>   Thy glory be our single aim!
> In all our intercourse below,
> Still let us in Thy footsteps go,
>   And never meet but in Thy name.

Separation from God

For I am persuaded, that neither death, nor life, nor angels, nor principalities, nor power, nor things present, nor things to come, nor height, nor depth, nor any other creature, shall be able to separate us from the love of God, which is in Christ Jesus our Lord (Rom. 8:38, 39).

No Christian—no sinner, for that matter—wants death to separate him from the love of God; but, comrade, the chief danger of separation between our hearts and God's love lies far, perhaps, this side of death; it lies in our life.

Do you allow anything to come into your life which makes you forget God, makes your spiritual life seem less real, and makes it absorbing interest wane, by ever so little? The events in your life over which you have no control will never affect you spiritually, except for the better; they are the provisions of God for your training and growth. But the things which are unlawful or inexpedient, and which you might alter or prevent if you liked, will surely put a distance between you and God.

I have seen a branch half broken from the tree retain a measure of life, but its beauty, symmetry, and strength were gone, and it bore no fruit. Do not let any fleeting trifles of this life separate you from the great heart of God. Consider the giving up of His life for you—both the foregoing of all human joys during His earthly existence, and the pouring out of His Blood upon the cross—and see if you can disregard such love, and bear a separation from it.

In every matter, great or small, be sure that your will is not God's side, for this constitutes true union with Him. You say your will is weak? Then side with Almighty power, for in that way only can it ever *rightly* become strong. The little brook which trickles down into the ocean gains no new force for itself from the union, but is lost in the vast tide. Yet, when a great wave comes curling up, carrying everything before it, the little brook drops are there; they mingle with the wave, they contribute to its power, and, were they sentient, would feel the joy of victory.

Life and its circumstances are not meant to separate us from God; they are simply the opportunity to merge ourselves in Him, to become hid "with Christ in God."